Miracle Grow for Business

Part of the Survival To Success Series
www.successfanatic.com
Luann Allen
Copyright 2011

Dedication

This book is dedicated to all of my clients, from whom I have learned so much, and to Mark, who always supports me when I'm too weary to keep going.

Table of Contents

The Author's Story 7

Introduction 9

Chapter I

The Well Planned Business 13

Goal Setting 21

Core Values 25

Business Plan 28

Research 32

Chapter II

Finding Your Client 37

Who Are You 41

Who Is Your Customer? 45

Chapter III

Talking About Your Business Easily 49

Marketing Components 50

Branding Yourself 54

Target Market 55

Bulls eye Market 56

Speaking To Your Avatar 63

Your B&B Statement 65

Chapter IV

New Business Basics 69

Location 71

Telephones 73

Website Basics 77

Business Cards 82

Contact Management Software 83

Accounting Software 85

Chapter V

Marketing Basics 87

The Cost Of Acquiring Clients 94

Trust Building Systems 97

Miracle Grow Touch Choices 104

Miracle Grow Touch Modalities 105

Miracle Grow Touches 110

Chapter VI

The Most Important Miracle Grow Touch Methods 115

Networking 116

Referrals   126
Demonstration   147
Give Aways   154

Chapter VII
Other Important Bulls eye Touch Methods
Direct Contact   147
Indirect Contact   168
Publicity   174
Keeping In Touch   180

Chapter VIII
Conclusion   189
Late Addition   193

The Author's Personal Story

My name is Luann Allen, and I felt that you should know my story, to understand why I wrote this book.

Twenty two years ago, through an odd act of fate, I was banished to a lovely little town in north Florida called St. Augustine. I had been living in Palm Beach County– an incredible wonderland for a girl who grew up in the farmlands of Pennsylvania.

There was culture and shopping, beautiful waterfront and gorgeous homes and estates in Palm Beach.

On the other hand, St Augustine is the oldest city in the country. Its claim to fame is that they have the oldest everything in the United States.

When I lived in South Florida, I worked like a maniac to lift my lifestyle so I could enjoy just a small sample of what the Palm Beachers had. I was young, energetic, thin, and loved my lifestyle. I was also incredibly stressed. I spent all of my time in Palm Beach in the restaurant and hospitality business, and although the money was terrific, the business was tough.

My health suffered, and my doctor suggested that if I didn't stop doing everything I was doing, I would die at a very young age. He firmly insisted that I didn't want to wait to change my lifestyle. It scared me. I realized that I needed to consider a change.

So I looked around, and thought St Augustine had charm. We had friends who lived here, and so, unlike the Beverly Hillbillies, who went into an *affluent* area, we loaded up and moved north, to an area that is less affluent than Palm Beach. Many of us refer to it as South Georgia, because if you have lived in South Florida, it doesn't feel like the same state. That is not to say that it doesn't have its advantages, because it does. It's a great place to raise kids and it can be very peaceful, but for this big city girl, to say that it was a cultural shock is an understatement of enormous proportions.

St. Augustine was a smaller town in those days, with a population of around 50,000 for the entire county, which translated to being a tough place to make a living. I wasn't used to that concept. It doesn't have a major shopping mall to this day. Palm Beach had a population of 1,000,000 +

when I left. It was an easy place to design a niche – you just had to open your doors, announce who you were and what you did and your customers would appear like magic.

I had to learn new rules and no one seemed willing to help me. It was a difficult transition for me. The natural thing seemed to be to try to appeal to all 50,000 residents. I was afraid to miss one because I needed the business. I floundered, but didn't fail. I made more than enough money, but I wasn't as successful as I wanted to be. I just couldn't seem to really get there.

The county started to grow and I watched new people come into town, opening businesses and being more successful than I was. Now my excuses about this little town didn't comfort me anymore. I wanted to believe that it was because I was an outsider, but the thought persisted: If other new people could do it, why couldn't I?

To add to the fun, I developed a couple of health issues. One night, while I was out taking my 4 mile daily walk, I heard a noise, even though I had my IPod on full volume. I realized that if I could hear it over the IPod, it had to be interior, coming from inside my body. I took about 6 steps and fell to the ground in pain. I had just experienced the explosion of the cartilage in my left knee. It was the last time I would walk unassisted for almost 2 years. During that two year time period I also had a heart malfunction and had heart surgery. Now I was in trouble. All of my savings dwindled to nothing and I had no security left.

It was time for me to stop fooling myself and find out why some of these business people were so successful. I set out on a mission to figure out what I was doing wrong and how to fix it. There were plenty of other service professionals like me, not only in my town, but all across the world. I knew it because I met them when I traveled to seminars. I started to describe myself as an education junkie, because no matter how much I learned, I still didn't have the whole story. I met many likeminded business owners who were searching for the same answers

What you'll read here are the results of my personal journey, incorporating what I learned by experience and from many experts into a systematic approach to building a business that really works. You can reach me by email at luann@successfanatic.com or go to my site at http://www. successfanatic.com

Introduction

Where Are You Now And How Did You Get To This Point?

Those of you reading this book will be at different points in your business life. The really lucky ones will find this book as they are beginning to plan their service business. If that's your situation, then congratulations! You are smart enough to know what you don't know and to want to fix it at the lowest cost possible. By doing some research before you begin, you've saved yourself thousands of dollars in lost revenue and wasted advertising costs.

Every year thousands of service professionals who work for other people decide that they can open their own company. If that sounds like you, then reading this book will let you evaluate your situation honestly so that you can weigh the pros and cons and make an informed decision before you jump out of the protective pan and into the fire. There's nothing wrong with jumping into the fire as long as you're prepared for it. A fire suit, water, fire extinguisher, etc. are all great tools to take with you so you can master the flames that will erupt in your business. No matter whom you are, things may get a little hot sometimes, unless you aren't doing any business. The heat is good for you: it keeps you from becoming frozen into inaction.

For those of you who have been in business for a while, you might be in a situation where you are realizing that you've basically bought yourself a job by investing all of your money in this business venture. You all know what I mean: you make enough to stay alive, but you aren't getting wealthy the way you thought that you would when you first started out. You don't really understand why. You blame it on the fact that you don't have enough time. You call yourself lazy for not working harder and longer. You blame your customers for being cheap or for not paying you. You blame the marketing gods for not seeing you and helping you to be successful. Some of you will even say that it's because you really don't care about the money.

No matter what stage you are in, it is time to throw a little Miracle Grow on your life to help both you and your business to grow. I'm here to tell you that if you grow your business, you and your life will also grow to be better and happier. So let's get started.

Read Once, Then Go Back and Make Your Plan

I suggest that you read this entire book first, then go back through and start planning. As you read, you will make unconscious decisions about what you are willing to do, and what you don't want to do. Ignore that little voice that's making those decisions. After all, you are the boss and you can override listening to anyone, even your own negative voice. We all have at least one negative voice inside that can hold us back so that we never have the things we want. You need to take charge and find ways to get things done. And believe me, YOU CAN DO THIS! If you fight yourself and lose, how can you ever win against the world?

Just make the decision to be a success and decide to read this entire book. That's when you'll be ready to do the exercises that I have for you at the end of the chapters. This will help you to develop a business and marketing plan that you can use as your business bible.

Those of you who are reading this and have been in business for a while – some of you for a long while - may be ready to admit that there must be a better way to do business, or at least an easier way. I promise you that there is a better way – more profitable and easier – to do business that they way you've been doing. I know because I've done it your way.

My aim is to help you to increase the number of clients you have, while receiving a higher hourly rate. I want your clients to be calling you so that you never have to worry about money again.

If you follow my instructions in this book, together we will change the way you do business forever. By implementing the principles in this book you will:

Increase the number of clients you have.

Increase your hourly rate.

Become known as the expert in your market so that you are respected.

Never be asked to cut your rates.

Have a successful business that you will someday be able to sell.

Boost your website copy so that your visitors know when you are talking to them.

Increase visits to your site by getting better Google placement!

Learn some basic article writing skills that will help promote your business

Find ways to develop additional income that can pay a large percentage of your basic overhead.

Impress the people you meet by describing your business in one powerful sentence

Plan specific hours each week to use for marketing.

Save money by knowing more about your how your business runs without you even being there.

Implement some basic financial and organizational forms that you can use to track your   business.

Have a short business plan that is realistic and sets specific goals both for the short term and the long term.

Brand your business well so that you can easily develop a vibrant, specific marketing plan

Plan your marketing to get the most bang for your buck.

Chapter 1

The Well Planned Business

Are You A Reluctant Business Owner?

Sometimes service professionals dream about going into business on their own, but sometimes they just kind of fall into their business. By that I mean that they did the same work for another company, and something happened to force them to go out on their own. So one day they wake up and realize that their lives have gotten much more complicated. Now, instead of having one boss, who paid them every week no matter what happened, they have as many bosses as they do clients, and they are never sure about whether or not they will be able to pay the bills.

It may be that they started doing some work on the side and they were really good at it. They were so good that they were under pressure from either their family or their newfound clients (which they may have stolen from their employer) to go out on their own. Without thinking about all of the cons of owning their own business, they plow forward into unfamiliar territory. Even though it may be that this is not what they really want to do, they open their own business.

It may be that they were laid off and found that so distressing to be tossed out after they've given their employer so much that they reasoned that if they go out on their own, they would never have to worry about losing their job again, because they would be in control of where and when they work.

Maybe they resented their boss and decided, in their great wisdom, that they were doing all the work and the business owner was making all of the money, and on top of all that, they got yelled at for not being perfect, even though they were out working while the boss was sitting on his boat doing nothing. They devised a concept, without any research, that they would just cut out the middle man (the business owner), charge less, and still make more than they were making working for that horrible rich person. This is the first example of someone not knowing what they don't know. How many of these people would actually love to go back to just working at what they love without the stress of worrying about money and employees all the time?

I must add one more example to this category as a result of the soaring unemployment rates that are now gripping our country. That is, the unemployed and seemingly unemployable who cannot get a job in their previous field and need to find a new way to make a living. It is a scary time for them. Many of them should be starting to wind down in their careers. Instead, they spend their time learning what they can about their new field, and not much else, and believe they are ready to open their doors to their waiting customers. Unfortunately, they don't learn about managing their business, even though that's what a business owner really is – a manager.

For many of the people in the above categories, they almost never realize that they now have this other role to play. They've crossed that great imaginary line that will change their lives. They are no longer just service professionals. They are now "The Business Owner", also known as "B.O.". That puts them into a whole new category. They don't get to get out of bed in the morning and just go and do what is waiting for them. They now have to be the one to go out and find business, to plan some strategies to make their business successful. They can't just be good at their service. They now also have to be a good business person.

Some of these people really love the new status that they have. They get to say that they own a business. It seems like the ultimate accomplishment. Except that they go into it thinking that once the business is open, all the difficult stuff is done. They thought that once they sorted through all of the government requirements, they were done. Their belief is that they can just go on providing their service as they did before, except that now they get to keep all of the money.

They didn't understand that their role would be to find business. They thought that if they built it, people would come. They thought that their clients, friends and family would promote it for them. They thought their advertising would bring in all the new business they would ever need.

So much for what they thought. It doesn't work that way.

You Don't Know What You Don't Know.

Unfortunately for these service professionals, they don't know what they don't know. They may be great at what they do, but this business management stuff is not their area of expertise. As a former service professional who worked for someone else, I need to be honest about this. If you just want to provide your service, don't become a business owner. If you are really excellent at what you do and love it, think twice before deciding to become the business owner. You won't be seen the same way by your clients. You can't act the same way because you have new responsibilities. It is difficult when you need to divide your time between doing what you love, answering the phone, making deposits, scheduling your appointments, listening to other people try to sell you stuff, etc. If you don't like being a manager, don't own a business.

On top of that, you will now have to be the bad guy, the debt collector sometimes, and make them pay you as they promised. It may be that you need to charge them more than they want to be charged. They will be disappointed. Some, who ultimately just used your services because they thought they could get a "deal", won't use you again. Others will either be embarrassed or hurt because you had to call them to get paid. They felt that they were doing you a favor by giving you business when they could have used anyone to do the same thing that you did for them.

There are other issues that arise out of this. Your new customers, some of who" knew you when" you worked for someone else, and knew that you were good at what you did, will be disappointed because you didn't learn the administrative part of your business. They get mad if you don't remember to call them back. You have no idea that you forgot to call them. They want to be billed promptly and are annoyed when you surprise them with a bill months later. They've already forgotten that you had provided them with your service. All of this administrative stuff is a surprise to you, the service professional. You had no idea that there would be so much involved in running this little, easy business!

You will become a target for bottom feeders who think that since your overhead is lower than a big company, and since they can get to you directly, they can ask you to take a lower fee, no matter how low your fee already is. In about 60% of the cases, they will get it because you will need the business. Get ready, because these are the people who will take up a lot of your time and they expect to get it for free.

Exercise 1

What was your motivation in deciding to start your own business?

Look at your situation honestly. Do you really want to own your own business? If you do, list the reasons why this is your dream.

What made you decide to own your own business?

Write a short synopsis of where your business is now.

What have you learned that you didn't realize you needed to know? At the end of each chapter, think about this and make note of what you find valuable.

Failing To Plan Means Planning To Fail

If you're not growing, you're dying.

Ultimately you are the one who will be the one to grow your business. As the saying goes, if you aren't growing, you're dying. This was never more true than it is in business. You may have enough clients to stay in business right now, but things happen to clients; they move, they die, they decide to use someone else, they don't need your service anymore. For that reason, you always need to look around for new clients to replace them.

It is my aim to get you to be so good at what you do that your market will come looking for you, but that doesn't happen on its own. You need to work at it to get to that point. What most businesses think is that advertising will build their reputation to get them to that point. They don't understand that without a marketing plan, they won't ever have a cohesive marketing system to get them on track, feel good about their business, and about what they provide as a company.

Sometimes small business service professionals who go out on their own develop a marketing plan of sorts by accident, some never develop one at all. When you develop an accidental marketing plan, the truth is that everything you do is almost always trial and error, which is the most expensive way to learn. Sometimes you wander off in a totally different direction than the one you started toward, and several years later, you realize that you made a mistake by getting pulled away from your original plan.

Marketing strategies are generally pretty basic, and generally common sense, unless you choose not to use them or plan them. If you are learning as you go, you will find yourself graduating from the School of Hard Knocks. The tuition will be high. Instead, do it right from the beginning. Make a marketing plan that will work with your abilities. For each person it will be a little different and will depend not only on your market but also on your own strengths and your comfort level. In some instances you might find that you will need to step outside of your comfort level, especially in the beginning, but the rewards will be beyond your wildest dreams, as you enjoy the fruits of your labor.

Business and Marketing Plan

If you don't have a business and marketing plan, this is the time to make one! We will be working on this indirectly in this book. When you are done, you will have a treasure map that will guide you to success. After all, if you don't know where you're going, how can you get there? Try to map quest a vacation with no destination and you won't get a map to show you where to go. When you travel without a plan, it might be fun and exciting for a while, but if you don't know anything about the area you finally stop in, chances are good that you'll miss a lot, because you didn't get to plan it out. Spontaneity is a wonderful thing, but not if you are building a business. When you have a plan, you can then decide whether you are on the right path or whether you need to veer off in another direction.

Besides knowing where you're going, you need to self-examine. Evaluate where you are and what you need in order to get to your destination. After all, map quest won't help you if you don't tell it where you're starting from. You must know your strengths and weaknesses, both as a business and a person. Otherwise you will try to do it all yourself, and that just can't work. Entrepreneurs are very well rounded by necessity, but it is impossible to have it all if you are trying to do it all.

So having a business plan means that you take a realistic look at every aspect of your business. Set benchmarks along the way so you'll know when you're making progress. This will help you to keep yourself motivated. Set short term (6 month) and long term (1 year, 5 year, 10 year and even 20 year) goals. Initially, as you use this book, set a 30 day and 60 day goal. Most people who are not looking for financing never really develop a strong business plan because they think that they don't have to have one. I am here to tell you that just because you don't have a banker asking for your plan, you will still need it. It doesn't have to be a formal 30 page business plan. **It can be very concise, provided it is precise, even if it is only hand written and a few pages.** It should include the who, what why, where and when on the industry you are planning to work in, meaning:

- Who you will sell to
- What will your products be
- Why you do what you do
- What geographical area will you cover
- When will you provide these services
- How will you provide these services

Then add your goals, including specific revenue goals, product goals, marketing goals, and growth goals. We will talk more about setting good goals in the next section, but for now, just know that you need to have all of this figured out, not just in your mind, but written out on paper before you start off on any path.

Exercise 2

On a scale of 1 to 10, with 1 being hopeless and 10 claiming expert abilities, rate yourself in the following areas:

Management abilities

Administrative experience

Bookkeeping skills

Computer skills

Writing ability

Resource location

Time management

Self motivation

Social skills

Decision making

Personal likability

Take a good look at the way you've answered the last question. If you've answered it honestly, you will see the areas where you need help. Start thinking about what you can do to improve in any area where you rated yourself 6 or less. Make a list of those improvements here and schedule time to accomplish them.

Start to work on your business plan. You won't be able to do it all right now, but do your best to answer the who, what, why, where, when and how questions in this chapter. List your answers below.

List some preliminary goals .

    30 day

    60 day

    6 month

    1 year

Goal Setting

Now that you've written some preliminary goals, let's see if we can improve them. There are some very basic rules around setting goals. Setting good goals correctly is critical to reaching them.

The little chart above, tells you that your goals must be SMART. This will make it very easy to remember when you are checking the goals that you've written to be sure that you have set your goals properly.

First, your goals must be very **specific**. That means that you can just say that you want to grow your business. You need to explain exactly what that means. Will you make more money? Have more employees? Have more locations? Have more recognition?

Second, your goals must be **measurable**. You can't set a goal that says you want to make more money. It needs to be expressed as a dollar amount, not as a percentage. In other words, if you want to increase your business by 40%, then you need to calculate how much income your business had this year, then multiply that by 40% so that you can know how many dollars that will be.

Third, it must be **attainable.** If you don't have any ideas about how you can make 40%, if you don't have any ideas about where that business will come from, then you must look at what you have done in the past. Have you ever increased your business by that much? If you haven't, then you must be able to explain what methods you will use to do this, and how much each method will bring in.

Fourth, it must be **relevant.** It has to be in line with what you are currently doing. You can't decide to go off on some unproven tangent that you have never tried, that has nothing to do with your current business, and expect to reach that goal.

Fifth, it must be **time-bound**. There must be a deadline. Whether it is 30 days, 60 days, a year, five years, 10 years or 20 years. There must be a time limit.

You Need to Make How Much?

If you haven't already done this, you need to figure out the financial side of your business. You must know how much your business needs to earn to pay you and provide for your future. First, determine how much you need to cover your personal expenses. Then you need to add money for the future, time for vacation, health care, and some money that is liquid for emergencies. Don't go into this with the intention of borrowing.

Using the money is easy; paying it back can seem Herculean. It's better to stay conservative in the beginning of your business. If you don't, you will become stressed about your finances and it will take away from the positive attitude that you'll need to be successful.

Calculate your business overhead. You may need to shop around initially to get the right deals. Whenever we opened a new restaurant, we never invested in new equipment at the beginning. We bought good quality used equipment and upgraded as we needed to. There was always a chance we would need to adjust the menu, and would need a freezer instead of refrigerator, or vice versa. We bought the almost new equipment of others who hadn't succeeded.

As a matter of fact, there is a great story to be told here. We opened a restaurant with used equipment that we bought for pennies on the dollar when we opened. We also bought great insurance at the time to cover not only the furniture and equipment, but also loss of revenue if we were unable to open.

As luck would have it, one day while we were open, we had an extreme power surge. It was so extreme, that even after we shut down the main breaker for the building, the ceiling fans were still spinning and some lights were still blazing. It was as though the building was possessed by some alien force. It fried everything in the building. We were closed for a week or two while we bought all brand new equipment and did electrical repair, which our insurance paid for, and I believe that they collected back from Florida Power and Light, since it was determined to be their fault. We were able to also collect for the revenue that we lost.

If you are a service business, your rates are easier to calculate because all you need to do is list what you personally need and will spend. You don't need a brand new car or van. Use what you have if you can, or find something that is presentable but already depreciated to get started. Your biggest expense will be your rent and telephones, unless you have employees. Employees are always a major expense, but if they are making money for you, then it is a worthwhile expense.

Guy Kawasaki, author of *Rich Dad, Poor Dad,* states that assets make you money and anything else is an expense. Employees fit into this category. If they are truly making you money, they are an asset.

If you have a service business and calculate your service rate and it is more than you can command, you'll have two choices. You will either have to find other ways to make money, or you'll have to improve your abilities so you can command a higher fee. By "other ways to make money", I mean that you will need to find a way to make some passive income, by selling an additional service that is not time consuming for you. It can be something that a minimum wage employee can do that you can charge much more for. If you can't do this, then you will need to improve your own knowledge and immediately find a solution to your potential clients' problems.

To prevent yourself from suffering any undo stress, you need to be able to look honestly at where you are now, and set some long term and short term financial goals. These goals should be in alignment so that when you get to your first goal, the next one is on the same path, or at least reachable from that first goal.

Stay On Course

If you set goals in different directions, there won't be any natural flow to your business. If there's something that you're thinking about adding to your business, and it doesn't fit with the natural direction of your business, don't do it! Changing direction in midstream is never a good idea without being absolutely sure, after you've done your due diligence, that you are definitely doing the right thing.

I've seen a lot of business owners who are all over the map and want to hopscotch from place to place without any real connection between them. They start to go in one direction, then turn completely around and start doing something else. When someone calls you to do the first thing that you were doing, you will lose money because you aren't doing that anymore. In addition, you lose business, because people become confused about your identity. You'll lose a lot of momentum by doing that. I've watched service businesses from all areas do that in their careers. They spend all of their time starting and none of their time finishing. If you decide to make a change along the way, think it through thoroughly. Answer the following questions:

What am I sacrificing by changing direction now?
Is it something that I have the knowledge or skill to do?
What would it cost me to get the knowledge or skills?
Is this something that the market really wants and needs?

If I do this, is it honestly better for my company financially?

Is it better for me psychologically?

How much business will I lose that I've already acquired?

Which brings me to the other important aspect of your business plan.

Core Values

Although your family may not be listed on any corporate papers as your partner, it is your partner. Whatever is important to your family must be considered. When you are setting up your business, in order to be successful, your business must be in alignment with your core values. It must also be in alignment with your family's core values.

Core values are those things that you passionately believe are important. Perfect service is a core value. So is the belief that you must give your family all that you can financially. But suppose that your spouse/partner believes that family time is more important than financial affluence for the family?

Can you see how these might clash?

If you commit to long hours that take you away from your family and hurt your home life, it won't work, because you will resent your business for taking so much time away from your family while you are trying to support your family and provide for their future. You will always be in crisis, feeling guilty for not adequately taking care of your family or your business.

Over time, you will resent your spouse/partner for having unrealistic expectations, and if your business requires you to work a certain number of hours and you don't work because you've promised to spend specific time with your family, you'll resent both your family and your clients for causing your business to fail.

All of these things need to be considered and resolved up front. If you are in business and you are struggling with your core values, today is the time to sit down, look at your business, and figure out if you can fix it. If you are aware that your spouse/partner's core values are different than yours, you need to find a way to structure your business so that you can align your business to both your core values and your family's.

If you are already in business, and find yourself in this situation, try to find a way to work this out.

If you can't do it any other way, and this business is really your dream, sit down with your spouse/partner and/or family and be honest about the situation. Ask for their support and their help. Try to identify a time in the future and a way that you can change it. If you cannot get their agreement, you may need to give it up and start looking for some other way to make a living, or start a different business.

If you don't address this situation and be realistic, you'll be wasting a lot of time – and money – and never get your business to where you want it. You will also not ever have the happy home life that you want. This will wear on you. It is inevitable that in time, either your business, your family, or both, will fail. In many cases, both will fail. When one fails, it is human nature to blame the other. There is nothing more distressing to me than to watch all of this unfold.

Exercise 3

How much do you need to make? Go to http://www.successfanatic.com/ratedeterminator and fill in all of the fields to get an accurate hourly rate.

How do your rates compare to your competitors' rates? If you don't know, do some research to find out. List three of your competitors with their rates here.

What are your short term financial goals?

What are your short term progress goals for your business goals?

What are your long term goals (5years, 10 years, 20 years)?

What are your core values?

What are your spouse/partner's core values?

What will it take to align your business with your core values?

How does your family feel about your business? If there are negative feelings, how can you resolve these issues?

Business Plan

This is going to be easier than you think. If you want to know how easy it will be, pick up a piece of standard paper. Turn it over. Your business plan will fit on that piece of paper. Most people hear the word business plan and go into an absolute panic. You can almost see their hair stand on end when I bring it up. I have good news. It really isn't that difficult.

Let's start from the beginning by getting started on your business plan. This business plan won't be the complicated mass of papers and statistics that you would use if you were going to apply for bank financing. For your purposes, your business plan will be your road map to success. So first let's ask the questions:

What do you do?
How do you do it?
How many employees will you start with?
What type of employees will you hire?
What are the cost of your goods?
Where do you want to be in a year?
How about 5 years?
How about 10 years?
When do you want to retire?
How do you want to retire?

What are your needs and desires?

How much do you need to make in the time you will be in business?

Will you have a salable business?

What will your expenses be?

Are there less expensive ways to run your business that will give you more bang for your buck?

What is the cost of any products you will need to supply to your clients?

How much competition do you have per capita? (Per capita is average per person)

Why are you better?

I'm assuming for our purposes that you will not be using your business plan to apply for startup money. This plan is only for your own edification. It's something you can initially read every night and every morning to remind yourself of your direction.

If you would like a large, complete business plan that you will be able to use to find startup money, you can find templates for these at http://www.score.org/business_toolbox.html

Exercise 4

Answer all of the questions listed in the above section. If there are other considerations that you are aware of, please address them here. I have rewritten the questions so you'll have space for answers.

What do you do?

How do you do it?

How many employees will you start with?

What type of employees will you hire?

What are the costs of your goods?

Where do you want to be in a year?

How about 5 years?

How about 10 years?

When do you want to retire?

How do you picture your retirement?

What are your financial needs right now? List them here

How much do you need to make in the time you will be in business in order to retire as you wish?

Will you have a salable business?

How much do you want to be able to sell your business for? (As a rule of thumb, you can expect to get 7 times your net)

What will your expenses be?

Are there less expensive ways to run your business that will give you more bang for your buck? List some of those possibilities here.

What is the cost of products you will need to supply to your clients?

How much competition do you have per capita? List some of the possibilities.

Who will be your most likely competitor?

Why are you better than your competition?

Research

Answering the questions in the last area will give you a good start on your business plan. Now you just need to figure out how make your business successful.

Talk to an Expert

It will take some research to look at your competitors and other lateral equivalent business owners to find out what they are doing. You should have already identified your competition. Now you need to identify some lateral business owners. By a "lateral equivalent" I mean someone who does the same thing but is not a direct competitor either because they are in a different area, or their niche is different from yours.

Finding a successful noncompetitive business is truly the easiest way to figure this out. If you find someone like this, schedule a meeting with them, either by phone or in person. It can even be someone who does what you do in another geographical area if you are operating on a local level. You can search by city with your exact criteria to find some of these businesses. If they don't show up in Google, they are probably not the most successful in their area. I say that because if they are the most successful, they will usually show up in one of the first three spots on Google that is not a paid spot. Generally people will be talking about them, and they understand how to market themselves.

Another good way to find them is to attend trade shows or local group meetings or by referrals from people that you know outside of your area. This is a great way to find these experts because people generally like to talk about who they know. Start conversations not only with participants, but especially with those who are manning the registration tables and involved with the organizers of the show. Ask around and talk to others. They will tell you who the big guys are. They may even know their stories. After you hear about these professionals, go online and Google them. Find out if they really are as described. See if their ideas agree with your own.

If you find someone who you like, or whose business you like, try to know as much about them as you can when you approach them. Tell them that you respect their accomplishments and would like to talk to them to get some ideas for your business. Spend some time before your meeting and prepare a list of questions to ask them. Take a notepad and make lots of notes. You're getting a free education. Finally, thank them for their time and be sure they know that you really respect them. Don't be afraid to be enthusiastic, however, don't be falsely effusive. People know when you're being genuine and when you aren't. Finally, ask them if there is anyone else that they think would be beneficial for you to talk to.

Immediately send them at least a card thanking them for their time. If you know of something they would enjoy more, make the investment and get it for them. This is a great way to begin to build a relationship with him and to begin to build your network. If they have suggested something and you do it, call them, email them, or send them a note telling them that you've implemented their suggestion and if they have time, tell them about your results. Reinforce this relationship any time you can! It is rare that anyone actually follows advice, and they will be impressed with your determination. They will understand that you are willing to do whatever it takes to make your business successful. Don't be surprised if some of these contacts become lifelong relationships.

Research Your Market's Demographics

Next, spend some time learning about the demographics of your market. Make a general list of all of the possibilities for your services. There are many ways to do that. If you are a regional service professional, you can check with your local Chamber of Commerce. They always have a lot of statistics that can help you.

If you are global, wander around the Internet. Use keywords to find both competitors and potential clients. Ideally there should be some people looking for what you have to offer. Google Adwords can tell you if there is demand for what you have to offer. Look at how many competitors are there and see what their rankings are. If there are more than ten it will be difficult to get a good rank without spending a lot of money. You may want to alter your business plan to do something a little bit different. That means that you will need to get involved with some of the social sites to know what you can contribute to the global community.

Find a Problem That You Can Solve

First, check the Google and Yahoo forums to see if you can find a new twist and solve a problem for your market. Join Facebook, Linkedin, and Twitter. All of this is free. The biggest downside is that it can be very time consuming, but this is the time to know if your dream can become a reality or whether you should reserve it for when you're asleep and leave it as a dream, instead of bringing it to life and making it a waking nightmare. The correct way to develop any product is to first find a problem that you can solve, and then develop the product or service to fix it.

Look for groups related to what you want to do. Read their conversations and get involved in the discussions. You will know after a while whether or not you have something to offer. If you do, proceed. If not, you need to try something else. Don't waste your time following a path that will eventually dead end either on the edge of a cliff with no way to go except down in a hurry or back to where you started.

It's important that you can brand yourself to offer something that is different in some way than everyone else. For that reason, once you've decided that you have something to offer, you'll need to start researching your competitors to determine what makes you different from them.

As an example, there are thousands of Internet marketers out there. They all have something different to offer. They each have their own little area of expertise that they know better than anyone else. It's the same with any product you see advertised on TV – they all have their own twist on what they offer. What makes you different? Is it what you do? Is it the way you do it? Is it in a different form? What problem can you solve for your clients that no one else can? What do you do better than any of your competitors?

Exercise 5

Who are your closest competitors?

Who are the lateral business owners who you can imitate? (those who are in your industry that are the same size)

Define a few ways to approach these business owner(s) that you've chosen.

Begin to investigate what your market wants and needs that they can't find or don't have access to. We will go into this more later, but this is a great time to put your ear to the ground and start listening.

What can you do in your business that will be different than your competitor(s)?

Chapter 2

Finding Your Client

Who Do You Like?

Your first priority is to determine who you want to serve and what you can do for them. This, along with defining your market, is commonly known as branding. You can spend hours honing this one aspect of your business, and it is extremely important to your marketing. There is nothing more important, and I suggest that until you can answer all of the aspects of what we've talked about so far, you cannot move on. You will also find that this will evolve a little bit as your business ages and you become better at what you do, and at knowing what your market needs.

It's human nature to believe that you can build it and they will come, whoever "they" are. But let me tell you a secret. They won't come unless they know that you are there for them.

Remember the movie "Field of Dreams"? The lead character built a baseball field in the middle of the cornfields for a bunch of dead baseball legends. He did it because he liked these ball players. He researched them and knew enough about them to know that the baseball players were looking for a field. "They" (the dead legendary baseball players) knew that the baseball field was built for them. They showed up. No one else would have showed up to play at that field, so it was a good thing that it was branded for the dead guys! Then all of the people who wanted to watch the country's top baseball players of all time also knew to show up. Why? Do you really think that the neighbors wouldn't talk about the goofy guy who used his land to build a baseball field for a bunch of dead guys? Everyone was talking about it. Imagine watching the best ball players of all time playing together! It was better than anything you could see anywhere else. And they played for free! (Fiction is wonderful for movies and entertainment and sometimes educational purposes.)

You need to provide the same uniqueness for your business. I would suggest that your customers should be alive so they can communicate with you. It's just inmportant to research them as much as he researched the baseball players in *Field of Dreams*. Let's start by first choosing who you want as a client. It's important to do this because ....

If you like the people that you work with:
- Your life will be much happier
- Your days will go faster
- You'll want to work in your business more

If you have a client who makes your life miserable:
- It will carry over to your other clients.
- They will take up your time.
- They will cost you emotional and physical energy.
- You'll find yourself thinking about them not only during work hours but also during your   personal time.
- They'll cause you to lose sleep.
- They'll make you feel like a failure

Choose Your Clients

Choosing your clients is the same as choosing your friends. You probably don't consciously think about who you become friends with anymore. That's because as you were growing up, you mentally sorted through that until it became second nature and just seemed to happen naturally. They were people who made you feel good about yourself. You understood each other without a lot of effort. They were comfortable to be around.

Part of this process helped you delineate who you felt comfortable with based on their mannerisms. Another part was understanding their likes and dislikes, their characteristics, habits and beliefs. You knew what was important to you, and you probably wouldn't associate with someone who didn't share those same thoughts and feelings. In the case of your business, you'll probably need to give it some conscious thought initially. Think about either your current friends and associates or current clients and use them as a guide.

Define Their Characteristics

Define their characteristics. Settling for any client who is breathing and has enough money to pay you is not specific enough. For example, I like to work with people who are generally focused, energetic, catch on quickly and don't need a lot of hand holding. They must be ethical and honest. They must do what they say they are going to do. They must have a good sense of humor, be kind and open minded.

It's difficult when you are talking to a potential client to know about them before you start working with them. If you are in a service business where you will need to work one on one with a client, you'll avoid a lot of wasted time and heartache by addressing this now.

Obviously some of you will not have to work closely with your clients. If that's the case, you can move ahead to the next section.

If you will be working with a client in a One-To One situation, such as accountants, consultants, designers, etc., you need to develop a "Discovery Form". These are questions to ask your potential clients that will give you some clues about the client they are before you work with them. Email them the Discovery Form before you ever talk to them. This form should ask your potential client both very direct questions and some indirect questions that may seem to them to be unrelated, but will actually tell you their views on issues that are important to you.

Some examples might be:

What are you most proud of in your life?
Where do you feel that you need the most help?
What qualities are you expecting from me?
What is the problem you are hoping to solve if we work together?
What goal do you hope to accomplish if we work together?
What has prevented you from reaching a goal?
Tell me about the best professional that you ever worked with? Why was he/she the best?
What specific expectations do you have of me?
How many of your goals have you reached in your life?

You don't want this list to be too long, because you'll get resistance from your client if the assignment becomes overwhelming for them. Generally, no more than 8 questions and no less than 5 questions seem to work best. However, if you are in a profession where you need to expect them to be very detailed and devoted, you may want to include a long questionnaire as a means of discovering if they are your ideal client. This can help you to decide if this client would be a good fit for you. Remember, that it only takes one unhappy client to make your life miserable. They will tell everyone about their bad experience. Nine times out of ten not only will they tell everyone about what you did wrong, they will embellish it so that they feel justified.

One unhappy client can ruin your reputation as "the best" at what you do.

Exercise 6

List the characteristics of the people you'd like to work with.

List traits you absolutely don't like in any person.

Develop some questions you can ask to learn more about a potential client.

Who Are You?

The next question you need to answer is:

Who is your business?

What is the personality of your business? We all have talents and things we're good at, and weaknesses and things we just can't do. So does your business. It's your job to identify all of that and to tell the world about it.

Most new business owners want to appeal to everyone. When you try to appeal to everyone, you end up appealing to no one. Go back to your days in school. The most popular kids were the ones who were much defined and didn't care if everyone knew it. They didn't worry about pleasing everyone. Your business needs to be just like that.

You must know who you are before you can tell anyone else who you are. Don't be afraid of losing business by doing this. If you aren't defined, you will find yourself with disappointed clients and here's why: (This is a special secret so lean in close and listen carefully.)

Do only what you do best.

If someone has expectations of you that are not what you are expecting or able to give them, there will be problems. You will say these are communications problems, but they will really be company identity problems.

Sometimes people will make an assumption about what you do. They think your business is something it's not. One of the biggest problems I've seen around this comes from the client expecting more than they get. It's because you aren't on the same wavelength. You think that you are providing a service as Items 1, 2, and 3. They think that you are providing Items 1, 4, 6, 8, and 9. Although you are familiar with those items, they are not your area of expertise and so they are not things that you normally consider doing. But you didn't define your identity. Your client thought he was getting someone else. Now you have a problem. You can't do what he asks. There are two scenarios.

One, you tell him that what he wants isn't an area that you are fluent in. If you're an attorney maybe he wants you to understand tax law and you're a real estate attorney. You suggest that he speak to someone else that who knows all of the ins and outs of taxes. He isn't happy because he hired you thinking you would know the law and before you were sure about what he wanted, you agreed to help him. Now he thinks you're just trying to help your cronies make more money. He doesn't understand that you are doing him a favor by being honest about your limitation. You never said, or advertised, that you are a real estate attorney. He goes away unhappy. He may even know that he's being unreasonable, but he doesn't want to admit that he may have made a bad assumption and that he should have asked about your area of expertise. So he never gives you a referral.

Two, you try to help him and be everything to him. You don't want to admit to him that you don't know this area of law. You get him some answers, and don't charge him because you feel responsible. You know you weren't clear. It takes you hours, and even when you're done, he has more questions that you can't answer and he thinks you're just dumb. He not only never refers anyone to you, he tells everyone you're the worst person born since Jeffrey Dahmer.

If you try to appeal to everyone, you will appeal to no one.

This one thing hurts small service businesses more than anything else. The service professional doesn't get to build a thriving business as a result, and has to take on clients that he doesn't like. He doesn't do a great job for them either, because he doesn't like them, or because they expect him to do things that he can't do, and a downward spiral begins.

An undefined service professional will take on clients he doesn't like or can't serve well because he needs the money. As a result, this company will fail within 5 years.

These companies fail for one of two reasons.

One, they have so many dissatisfied customers that they don't get enough business to keep going. It's like the kid in school that nobody liked because he seemed lazy and always made excuses for his poor performance. If he weren't smart and admitted that he wasn't smart, people might try to help him, but he's handling it all wrong and coming across as though he just doesn't care. These companies can't market themselves because they know they don't make their customers happy.

Two, these business owners decide that all clients are horrible and they begin to hate all people because they reach a point of burnout that they can't recover from. They can't market themselves because they don't want to talk to "those" people. They especially don't like really successful people because they are forced to acknowledge that these successful people know something that they just can't figure out.

Whichever one of these happens, I find it to be one of the saddest things I've ever seen in my life. It's devastating because it doesn't just ruin their businesses. It ruins their marriages, because they feel like failures, and it ruins their lives because they don't trust anyone anymore. They become bitter and take jobs working for other people in other fields where they generally don't make as much money. They will tell you that they hate that industry. This could have been avoided if they had structured their business differently at any time during their business life. If you watch people who have been in business for a while and are failing, you will see that they just can't imagine changing the way they do business.

A big part of running your business correctly, along with verbalizing who you are and what you do, will be to state your services clearly and to be sure that in your initial conversation with your client, you are very clear about what you can and cannot give them for the fee you describe. We'll talk about this more in your writing strategy.

Exercise 7

Delineate your main service.

What problem will you solve for your client?

What is the scope of your work? Be very exact.

What does it not include?

What is the cost for this service?

Who Is Your Customer?

For now, let's get back to talking about who your customer is.

Sometimes it is easier to sit down and imagine your customer avatar.

If you are currently in business, you can probably think about some of your best or favorite clients. Close your eyes and visualize that person. What do they look like? If you are like most business owners, you can describe two clients, one man and one woman.

If you are new to business, think about the people that you get along with best. Is this someone who might be a client?

Describe that person in detail.

What is their age?
What are their needs?
What are their desires?
How do they talk about it?
Where do they find you?
Why do they look for you?
When do they need you?
When will look for you?
What language do they use to describe their problem?
How painful is this problem for them?

Put this information together with the information on your ideal client. Try to imagine exactly what your actual customer looks like. Blending these two will give you a clear vision of who you're serving. It may be someone you once worked with or someone you know who needs your services. If you have a picture of that person, keep it in front of you on your desk. It will help you stay focused on who you're looking for so you'll recognize them when you see them.

Exercise 8

Using all of the above information, design your customer avatar. This is not written in stone and can be altered with a little plastic surgery later if you need to, but you need a starting place.

What is their age?

What are their needs?

What are their desires?

How do they talk about it?

Where do they find you?

Why do they look for you?

When do they need you?

Where will they look for you?

What language do they use to describe their problem?

How painful is this problem for them?

Chapter 3

Talking About Your Business Easily

Marketing Plan

The purpose of having a marketing plan is simple. You always need to have clients, potential clients, and potential exposures to clients on your calendar. The reason for all three is simple: Even if your client calendar is now full, at some point in the future, you'll be done working with those clients and you'll have to fill your client calendar again. If you wait until your time with you current clients is over, you'll essentially be starting from scratch every time.

Many service professionals have no intention of doing anything except providing their service to clients. For that reason, they don't see why they need a business plan. They want to just wing it, play it by ear, trust in a higher power to provide for them, and hope for the best. Many will say that if it doesn't work out then it wasn't meant to be. Baloney!

I'm standing here in front of you and figuratively looking you in the eye to tell you that YOU NEED EITHER A BUSINESS PLAN WITH AN EMPHASIS ON MARKETING OR A COMPLETE MARKETING PLAN. You don't need one of the complicated ones that businesses use when they are applying for loans, but you need a road map for yourself and your one or two employees, if you have any, so you'll know who you are and have direction, a plan of attack, and a schedule to find new clients. You can use the simple two page business plan, but if you do then you need to do a more extensive marketing plan, outlining ever type of marketing you will do. When I talk about marketing, I'm not talking about just advertising. Advertising is only a part of marketing, and it's the secondary part. The biggest aspect of marketing is to delineate the way you talk about your business. Then you need to decide where, when, and how you will market.

Marketing Time

Nothing will be more important to your beginning business than spending time working on your business rather than in your business. This is why I am insistent that you schedule a specific number of hours every week to market yourself. That probably means that if you only want to work a 40 hour work week that you won't be able to work with clients for the full forty hours of a standard work week.

You must allow at least 5 to 10 hours per week to consistently market your business. In this way you will always have an active "pipeline". A pipeline is a series of future clients who you interest and who are at different points of needing your services. Many service professionals find they have a rollercoaster of business, and it is because they don't market consistently. What happens is that they market, then they get busy so they stop marketing, then they run out of business, so they market, but they get busy, so, well, you get the idea.

Marketing Components

There are four components to your marketing plan:

Marketing Web – This concept says it better than anything. My vision of this is that it looks like a spider web, and just as the spider allows bugs to come and get stuck and crawl around on his web until he's ready for a meal, your marketing should cause your contacts to "stick". This is the combination of active clients, potential clients, and new contacts that you want to have at any given point in time. They are somewhere in your field of vision, moving around on your marketing web, getting to know you and wanting to be there. They are enjoying the view and the breeze.

If you are an accountant, your marketing web may look like this.

You may have those who are just beginning a new business and are a few months away from being able to set up books.

You may have another who is thinking about changing accountants and you just need to wait until he decides that the time is right to change accountants.

You may have another one who you set up a few months ago, for a good sum of money, but he hasn't started generating enough revenue to pay you on a regular basis.

You go to an event and reconnect with one who is now ready to hire you with an annual contract.

One of your other clients call who has been using you quarterly and he wants to start having you track his books from your office on a daily basis by computer.

Marketing Strategies – These are the threads that you use to build your web. They are built out of the different methods that are available to market your business. You want them to be your best so they are strong and sticky and collect as many bugs as possible without breaking.

Since I spend a great deal of time discussing these later in the book, I won't talk about this a lot here, except that an example would be as follows: a combination of networking, direct contact in person, web strategy, direct contact by mail, scheduled phone calls, and writing a newspaper column in your local paper.

The combination will be different for every single person. I love to personally design these for different service professionals. We take into account the personality of the professional, the geographic area of the business, the nature of the business, and the specific talents of the professional.

Schedule of Events – A weekly calendar of events you will use to plan your marketing strategies which will get people into your marketing web. This schedule should include a way to track your results.

This is the specific form to develop so you can schedule where you need to be and when, and a specific time and day of the week for writing or phone calling or any other marketing requirement that doesn't have a set time. If you don't schedule it, you won't do it. (After you return from the event or make the phone call, you need to track the results of what you did. There should be room for that on your form.)

Continuing Client Goals – This is the number of active clients, potential clients, and new contacts that you want climbing around your web at any given point in time. Being vigilant and tracking these on a weekly basis will keep your bank account and your attitude moving up.

Your goals should list the ideal number of clients you will have at any point, and the amount the client will be paying. You may have 8 clients at $75, 12 clients at $100, and 8 clients at $125, all per hour and assumed to need one hour. This would be assuming that you need to average $100 per hour.

As you complete assignments with your low paying clients, you can raise those prices to $100, and gently raise your prices on a regular basis. In this way, even if your initial fees begin a little lower than you'd like them to be, you will have a system for raising them as you become better known and you gather more testimonials and satisfied customers.

Marketing Web

Sales professionals tend to use the term "sales pipeline" and "sales funnel". This is the same as a marketing web, and you must keep your web full to assure that you don't find yourself with high points and low points in sales, so that you will always have consistent cash flow. The term pipeline seems too flat. I like the term web because it can represent different products or services at different prices. Sales funnel usually indicate that they are buying higher dollar items as they go along, so it is not appropriate for service businesses.

You must have all of those possibilities out there in your sales web so that if you find yourself short a client and need money, you can approach these people to see where they stand. Someone may be ready to commit to you if you just nudge them a little. You also want to have functions to go to where you might meet a new client or get a referral for someone who needs you now.

This marketing web process, along with defining your business target market, (branding), is the most important part of your business plan.

Take plenty of time to work on the Bullseye Benefit Statement part of this book which is next. If you don't solve this now, you won't get full benefit of this book. For this reason, I am asking you to contact me at luann@ successfanatic.com if you can't devise an incredible Bullseye Benefit statement. I would be happy to help you through this portion. When I work with clients, I won't go any farther until this piece is firmly in place because I know that you can't succeed without it and it will ruin your business and your life. I can't emphasize this enough.

So, although you have clients now, you must have some new flies waiting in your web to become new clients. You must also have marketing in place that will give you an opportunity to expose yourself (clothes on) to new people.

Exercise 9

What is the total number of clients that you want to have at any one time?

What is the average rate you will be paid per hour?

How many clients will you have at each of your rates? Break them down here.

How many hours per week will be client hours?

How many hours per week will be marketing hours?

What will your marketing hours consist of?

Branding Yourself With Your
Bullseye Benefit Statement

If you've been around the net or exposed to any groups in the last few years, you've probably heard the term "branding". It is just as it sounds, cowboy. Heat up the fire, round up the herd, and get ready for some fun, because once you get really this concept, you can't lose. It will make it easy for anyone to describe your business, from your employees to family to people who meet you at networking events.

Branding is the method a business uses to identify who it is as a business. It originates from the business's chosen niche.

Choosing Your Brand

Remember what I said earlier? Everyone thinks of marketing as advertising or sales. That's not the case. Marketing is who you will appeal to and how you will tell them about your business. Advertising is the specific medium that you will use.

You really need to take some time to think through the way you want to describe yourself. It is this that will brand you – like M&Ms (melt in your mouth, not in your hands). Or Coca Cola which is "the real thing". But it is generally much tighter for a small company rather than something this general, because we can't compete on the same level. Be careful – if you don't choose your own brand, someone else may choose one for you, and it may be something that you really don't want to do as a specialty.

The smaller your company, the more specific your brand should be. I like to call them boutique businesses, because just like those exclusive little clothing stores, you need to be able to command the same high prices. You can command these prices by giving them something they can't get from Wal-Mart. I always suggest that the one thing you give them is not better service, because if you grow, that may be difficult to maintain. Better service in this case means that you are always attentive to their phone calls, which you don't charge them for, even when it's obvious that all they want is to speak with you. Great service is like the lowest price. It's a nice promise, but sooner or later someone else can come along and improve on your model. Instead, give them something that only you know how to do, and your customers won't even look at the Wal-Mart version of your competition. What you do for them can't be replaced by anyone else.

As a side note, sometimes someone will come along and try to do what you do, but in any product or service, the first one is the one that's deeply ingrained in the client's brain as THE one. Both Coca Cola and Google are great examples of this

So... let's get started inventing your brand.

Can we have a drum roll, please?

Target Market

A target market is the large group of the population who could need your services at any given time.

55

First, define your general target market. That is the group of people who can use your services. It is sometimes referred to as your niche.

For a plumber, that can be anyone who has or needs plumbing, whether it is drain lines or water lines.

That's pretty general. Although it sounds like that means you have a lot of potential clients, so does every other plumber. You really don't want to be just like every other plumber, because how will they choose you over everyone else?

When they look in the phone book, what will make you more appealing that everyone else? You can get a slight advantage in the phone book by naming your company something that will give you an alphabetical edge. This used to be the best strategy as part of your marketing arsenal. Now, it's a small part of it. You can buy an enormous ad and spend a lot of your profits, but keep in mind that phone books are not the preferred method for finding a business these days.

Having a good local web presence has become much more important. Most people don't use phone books any more. They go to the web – even for local help. There are directories on the web that list local businesses. On the web, you won't be listed alphabetically or have the biggest ad.

So how will you get attention?

You must narrow your niche, minimize your market, and trim your target, to get to your dead center market.

This is going to take some thought, so let's talk about it.

Bulls eye Market - What Only YOU Have To Offer To A Very Specific Group of People

A bullseye market is the narrowed down, very specific segment of your target market.

Now, narrow your target market down to what I call your Bulls eye Market. That is the subgroup of your target market that can only use *your* service, because you can fix some very specific problem for them.

Spend some time thinking about how you are different from the other people you know who are targeting your general target market. This isn't an easy thing for most of us to do, because we grew up trying to conform and be like everyone else and blend in. That makes for a mediocre business. In order to really stand out, we must demonstrate how we are different.

Start by making a list of what your competitors have to offer. Start with their marketing material. Then talk to their clients if you need to. Ask their clients what it is about them that they like? That they don't like? There may be an opening here for you to be better than your competition. Talking to the competition's clients can be very easy. You will run into them everywhere you go, in the grocery store, doctor's office, or church. They are easy to find. As you do this, you will hear a theme starting to develop for each one. That will tell you about their branding.

Ask these same people what it is that they want and can't find, or what problem that they have that they need to solve. This will help point you in the right direction.

Then, it is important to look at the image that you present to potential clients. Many businesses want to pretend that they are bigger than they are. I suppose that it makes them believe that the public will think they are more successful. You don't need to present yourself as big, but you probably want them to know that there is more than you. Think about where you will be for your company. Are you going to be your customers' problem solver? Or will it be your company? You can structure your business either way, but remember that if you put yourself out as the problem solver, you will have a difficult time ever selling your business in the future, because when you leave, the perception will be that the expertise has left. It also limits the amount of money that you can make, because you'll need to be on every service call. No one else will be good enough.

Back to finding your area of specialty. You've looked at what your competitors are doing, so now you can rule out specializing in what your competitors are doing. There is one exception here. If you can do it ten times better than your competition, you can do the same thing by putting a slight twist on it. As I said earlier, generally the first one to establish their reputation for doing something specific is the one who gets to keep the title unless you have some small valuable thing to add to it. It may be something simple that makes the customer's life just a little easier. A plumber who can take a credit card will do better than a plumber who only wants cash or checks.

Think about what you can offer clients that your competitors either can't or don't offer. It can be something small or something big.

For instance, there are some carpet cleaners who advertise that they are the little guy who will agonize over every single stain in your carpet (they don't say it that way of course), or the one who gets out pet odors. Then there is the big guy who brags about the water extraction they can do because they have a big machine. Is one better than the other? It depends on the needs of the client at the time he hires a carpet cleaner. If you need water extraction, then you'll call the water extractor. If you have a smelly dog, you will want the odor man.

I know a plumber who advertises his year round service plan to keep drains clean. Pay him an annual fee and have clean drains for life. His competitor advertises the lowest price. Lowest price, by the way, is never the right thing to do. Someone else will always come along whose prices are lower.

If you don't believe that, think about the airlines who have tried to open over the years. Ten dollars a flight to the first ten people. They lasted in my town for eight months before they had to go out of business.

Remember the Five and Dime? K mart came along and seriously hurt them, now Wal-Mart is doing the same to K mart. Wal-Mart has taken this a step further, and seriously beats down their suppliers, which most other companies can't do because they don't have the same power that Wal-Mart has because they are so large. I won't give you my opinion of Wal-Mart here. That's an entirely different subject and since I represent a lot of "Mom and Pops", I resent what Wal-Mart has done to small business in America. I know that Wal-Mart has its place in our society, and that many low income families rely on Wal-Mart for low prices to stretch their dollars, but I believe that if they could take my job and do it cheaper, they probably would. In the long run, I'm not so sure that it's good for our economy to take away small businesses.

Aside from your standard fare or lower prices, which I've just shown to be a bad idea, what else can you offer your client? In the old days, back in the 1970s, I lived in upstate New York for about 5 years. Since I was a marketing person, I had a job working for a heating company. The company had telephone sales people who would make appointments for technicians to go in and check the customer's furnace every fall before the cold weather came along. These were not necessarily current customers. I had a phone bank of five people who made cold calls. Since it was a free service, it wasn't difficult to book appointments. Sometimes they would find repair items that needed to be addressed. Sometimes they didn't find anything. It always made the homeowner feel warm and cozy, not just because his heat was working, but because he felt reasonably certain that if there was something wrong, the company would have found it so they could make money on it. If something did happen, guess who he called? You guessed it. He called my company because he trusted us.

You can also provide a low cost service that will bring you some additional easy money over the course of the year. I live in Florida, and some air conditioning companies will give you a contract to come and service your unit twice a year for a fixed fee. It also includes a discounted price off emergency service. As another add on, they will come out and change your air filter 4 times a year. They have a woman who gets paid $7.50 an hour to change filters. They charge $25 for the service so even after the cost of the filter and travel expense; they are still making about $10 per filter change. It's great in our elderly Florida economy for all of the senior citizens who are unable or unwilling to mess with changing their own filters. This is a great way to guarantee that when the big ticket item needs to be purchased, they'll stay with the same company because they trust them. This is relationship building at its best, because if you live within one mile of the ocean, you will need a new system about every 5 to 8 years.

I have a friend who does computer repair. He has taken it to another level. He doesn't just take your computer and fix it, he monitors it remotely to tell you ahead of time when you might be close to having problems so you can address the problems ahead of time. He can also advise you about how to install a backup hard drive so you never lose what's on your computer. If you want him to do it, he will back it up onto his server so it will never be lost. He's different because he doesn't wait until you're desperate for help. He gives you an alternative, and peace of mind. This is now being done by many IT companies. It provides them with passive income on a monthly basis, and when you need new or additional equipment, they will buy it from the same company.

If You're Stuck

If you can't think of anything that makes you different from everyone else, You are probably thinking that there is nothing different under the sun. You are wrong. There is always something different. If there weren't the same companies would be the only ones to be in business for centuries. If you don't see one available, you'll have to invent a way to be different.

First, make a list of what you competitors currently offer. That will give you a great start. This may trigger an idea or you might find a hole that you can fill. If you can't think of anything different, go online and do a search in noncompeting areas and see what they are doing that you might be able to do. For example, if you are a Dog Groomer in Detroit, take a look at what dog groomers in Cleveland are offering. Go to Google and type in "Dog Groomers Cleveland". Read their websites to see what they are doing. You might find one who travels nationally to dog shows with their clients. I'd bet you'll find someone you can model by doing this exercise.

Find some online forums and groups and join in the discussions. See what issues they are presenting that you have an answer to. If you are already in business, ask your current clients what they would like to have that they don't have now. This may take some time to figure out. If you really pay attention and work at it, it may take just a day or two to formulate your idea. When you find the people who present the problem that you know you can solve, makes some notes. Listen to the way they describe the problem. Make notes of the language they use. When you write your copy later you'll want to be able to appeal directly to them.

Once you have your idea, think it through carefully. Look for flaws. Carefully ascertain that your competitors aren't doing the same thing. If they are, it isn't a crisis. It doesn't mean that you can't do it. It just means that you'll need to find a new or better twist that your clients will find appealing. What can you do to improve on the idea? Visualize all the motions of performing the service. Visualize yourself doing it. See your customer. What other problems arise as you are providing the service that you can capitalize on? What do you see that you do for your customer that your competitor doesn't do? For example, if you are an electrician, and you go out to install a new circuit breaker, what do you do at that time that is not part of the repair? Do you check other aspects of the electric system? Can you suggest a whole house surge protector to protect the consumer from having this happen again? Can you do a basic electrical check to ascertain that their system is working properly? Is there a device that you can use to look for hot spots inside the wall that might lead to an electrical fire due to poor wiring? Maybe you can make some great suggestions that will help them to save big money on their electric bills. I must add that you might really have to put some work into discovering what this will be for you.

Whatever your idea is, cement it into your brain, which is just the right place for it. This will become the nucleus of your new business. Dream about it. Write it out. Concentrate on how to describe it as a problem solver for your clients. You should be able to describe it in one sentence. It is what you will say to anyone who asks you what you do for a living. It is something you should be able to say in your sleep and when you're so tired you can't function. Much like the Dunkin Donuts man (time to make the donuts).

This will be your identity.

Exercise 10

Who is your target market?

Make a list of every possible aspect of what your business can do.

What can you do really well or what can you learn how to do really well? What will you become an expert at?

Ask either your current clients or potential clients to tell you about a problem they might have. List it here.

How you fix this problem or provide them with what they need?

Go to the online forums and see what people are talking about along these same lines. List these issues here.

If they aren't talking about any specific issues, ask them if there are any issues that they have around your industry that you could help with. List them here. Be sure to ask if anyone else has the same problem. You must know that you have enough demand for the service. Make a list of these issues here.

What is your specialty?

Who are the clients who need this service? They are your bullseye market. Name them here.

When do they look for you?

Describe the problem you fix and who your bullseye market is.

Speaking To Your Avatar

In the basic version of your "whom", you described your customer. Now that you know your "what" you can be more detailed about your "whom".

This is your customer avatar. In case you don't spend much time around video games, an avatar is kind of a caricature cartoon character. In this case, it is a picture of who your customer is. It is your perfect customer in your Bulls eye Target Market who needs exactly what you have.

You had an earlier exercise where you delineated this person. Now you want to get to know them intimately. Provided that you've done your homework properly, you've probably already spoken or written to this person. You have notes on the language they used and the way they described the problem and their difficulty in finding a solution. They may have talked about all the things they tried that didn't work. You may know what they do for a living, or how old they are, or how many kids they have. All of these things need to be embedded in your thinking, so that when you are marketing your business, whether in person or in writing, you can speak directly to them.

You even want to know when they have their third cup of coffee during the day, or the fact that they only eat organic foods and never eat sugar. Whatever it is, you want to know them as well as you know your best friend.

For example, a client may say to you:

"I wasted so much time on this one thing that I missed a deadline on a project. The client was furious and just fired me. If I had help getting this done, my business would be different. I would be more successful, less stressed."

"My lack of direction is killing my business. I keep starting different things and spinning my wheels and I never get anywhere."

You have a picture of them on your desk. Now imagine you can hear their voice. Let them talk to you during your planning time. Periodically ask them questions and listen to their answer. In *Think and Grow Rich,* Napoleon Hill regularly talked to his mentors and they came to life for him. Your clients need to do the same.

Speaking to them gets to be very easy when you know them so well. Over time you will know them as well as your best friend, or a member of your family. It will become normal to talk to them, and you will learn what their strengths and weaknesses are as your "relationship" grows. Read Napoleon Hill to understand this visualization technique better.

Exercise 11

What does your customer say when they talk about their problem or their need?

What effect does this have on their lives?

What is the pain caused by not having this solution?

What do they see as their direct benefit of solving this?

Your Bullseye & Benefit Statement
-Putting It All Together

Now you know who your perfect client is. You know who you are as a business. You also know your target market and your Bulls eye Market. Last, but equally important, you know what problem you solve for your clients, and you know what you can do for your client that your competitor can't or doesn't.

That gives you the basis for a powerful one sentence description of whom you are that you will be able to use when someone asks you what you do. Rather than saying I am an accountant, or I own ABC Accounting, you will be able to say "I help clients to hone their finances so that they will be able to retire in comfort when they are ready" or " I bird dog my clients financials closely to help them eliminate waste and be aware of potential money losing situations before they become a problem".

Isn't that more interesting? Wouldn't that open up a conversation with someone who had that concern?

To make this process easy, try stating it by first saying "I help…" then add the who and finish with the benefit to the client, which may sound like "so that". This becomes your perfect one sentence mission statement which I call your B & B Statement (Bulls eye and Benefit). As another example, "I help service professionals learn a new way of looking at their futures so that they can live the life they've always dreamed of".

So put on your superhero cape, add your wizard's thinking cap and generate 5 or 6 different versions. Try a different one out each time you're introduced to someone to find the one that seems to generate the most interest and gets the most results. Write it down and repeat it until you now it as well as your name. As time goes on, it will probably evolve a little. You may even find that in different groups, you may use another description for who you help and what you do for them. That's to be expected. Don't block it out. Many business owners tell me that they don't just do one thing well. They have a couple of different types of clients. In the beginning, I don't suggest that you do this because you may use the wrong identity at the wrong time, but I am aware that it happens frequently. You must just be aware that you don't want to dilute yourself until you build a reputation for being an expert in a specific area.

Exercise 12

List 6 different versions of your B & B Statement.

Use each one with at least 6 people. After you use each one, list it here along with the results that you received when you used it.

Chapter 4

New Business Basics

This section has been added for new businesses to help them do things in a logical order and to help them save time. It is also beneficial for established businesses to be sure that you have all of your bases covered.

Where To Begin

Before you go anywhere and start talking to anyone, there are some basic things that you need to get done to showcase your business correctly the very first time. This book assumes that you will take care of any governmental requirements as you set up your business.

The basic items that you will need to accomplish are as follows:
Business Hours
Telephones
Location
Logo
Domain Name
Website
Business Cards
Contact Management Software
Accounting Software

Determine Your Hours

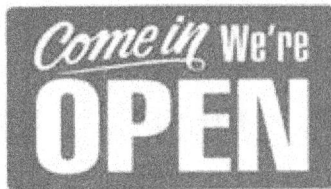

Your Hours of Operation are the hours when you will officially take calls from clients or potential clients, and when you will potentially schedule time with clients. Unless you have help, you have to allow time for answering calls and talking to clients.

In some businesses, you have the luxury of scheduling specific times to answer and respond to calls. You can schedule regular times every day when you check messages, and turn off the phone the rest of the time.

Some service businesses don't have that option. If you are a real estate agent, and you don't take the phone call immediately, you will probably lose the client. In some businesses, when you don't answer, they are on to the next professional. This generally happens to general service people rather than those who specialize. RotoRooter, for example, has the market cornered on excellent drain cleaning. Most people will give them a chance to call back before they move on to another plumber.

Client Hours are the number of hours you will actually spend with clients which are also known as billable hours. If you only want to work a 40 hour work week, you won't be able to work with clients for the full forty hours of a standard work week. As you remember, you must allow at least 5 to 10 hours per week to keep marketing your business. In this way you will always have an active "pipeline". As defined earlier, a pipeline is a series of future clients who you interest and who are at different points of needing your services. You also need to allow for about 5 hours of administrative time, unless you have an assistant. This will be time when you make notes about clients, complete and send invoices, make phone calls for supplies, etc.

Your marketing time is a critical part of your business and deserves your attention both in the beginning and as your business progresses and you need to periodically reassess what works and what doesn't work. If you keep good notes you will be able to track what portions of your marketing works, and what can be deleted. Sometimes we think something is working, until we track it.

Exercise 13

List your complete hours of operations.

List the hours you will be available to clients

Location

First you need to decide on a physical location for your business. I won't spend time on how to choose a physical location, except to talk about the virtues of outside office versus home office.

For some professionals, it may be possible to work from a home office. It depends on what you do and local zoning laws. Working from home can save you a substantial amount of money provided that you can work without distractions. Many people find that it is much too easy to have your time diverted by household chores and family issues if they work at home. Others are very focused and have found that if they set up rules for themselves and their families that it can work quite well.

It is also limiting to your company to work from home. If you hire someone, you may not want them in your home, particularly if you have outside appointments. You may have a noisy dog, a screaming child, or someone else in the home that requires your attention when you need to concentrate on your business. If any of these things are present in your home, you will want an outside office. You will make up the money that you spend on rent.

It is also nice to have a location with a sign. This billboard can get you a substantial amount of business, and invites potential clients to check you out. It also makes you much more accessible to the general public, because they can stop in to your office and see you during your business hours. It also makes people feel more secure about your stability as a business.

I have always had an office outside my home. I liked the definition of "going to work" and knowing that was my time to devote just to my industry. When I decided to move my business into my home, it took some time to adjust and set up rules for myself, my daughter, and the family dog. One of the biggest challenges was finding myself on the phone with a client and having someone knock on the door. The dog would bark, the bell would ring and I was trying to be cool and calm and pretend that none of it was happening. I finally had a sign made that said: "I am currently with a client. Do not disturb" for outside on my front door. There will be issues to solve if you work at home, so I generally suggest that new businesses rent office space, at least for a while. It doesn't have to be large space; it just needs to be separate so you can focus.

The other problem with working from home is that you are always at work. It's too easy to find yourself with an extra 30 minutes in the evening, so you start working and then your family feels ignored, and you can feel that you never get away from work.

Working from home does make networking and a website even more important so that you don't become isolated, which can easily happen. Isolation may be good if you're writing a book and don't want to be disturbed, but it won't help you get new clients.

Exercise 14

List all of the pros and cons of working from home, including any zoning laws that you need to adhere to.

Calculate how much space you will need for an office.

Telephone

Nowadays you don't see vanity phone numbers. Vanity numbers are phone numbers that you request so that your phone number will be memorable. They generally tell people something about your business. I always thought they were wonderful. When I had my real estate company, my phone number ended in SELL. The phone carriers have stopped taking requests for vanity numbers. It is possible to still get vanity toll free numbers and you can do that on the Internet, but be ready because it can be expensive to "buy" that phone number.

Will you need a toll free number? Will your clients be only in your local area? If you need a toll free number, you can either get one through your provider, or you can go online. There are quite a few providers online who will provide toll free numbers starting at $9.95 per month. At last check, AT&T would provide one for $5 per month. It depends on your needs and the usage it will get since there is a per minute charge.

You need to decide whether you'll have a land line or just a cell number. If you have only a cell number, I suggest that you get another cell for personal calls. If you don't keep them separate, you will always be answering your work phone and working whether you want to or not. In many cases it can cause you to appear unprofessional.

You'll want to think about after hours calls. How will they be handled? Do they require an immediate return call? This will depend on the nature of your business and what you tell your clients. If you are a repair business, you will probably want to have some method to handle these calls.

A dog groomer won't have emergencies. No dog needs an emergency haircut UNLESS he's in a show tomorrow and he rolled in gum this evening. Neither will an accountant, unless he specialized in IRS audits.

A plumber will need to plan his after hour calls. Do you hire a service? Take care of all of these calls yourself? Maybe you can split the cost of the service with another plumber. If you have an employee, you may split the evening emergency duty with him, and make sure that you have a way to either forward calls to the appropriate person or have a separate cell phone that the one in charge will have. You may decide that you don't want to do after hours calls. In that case, you need to go back to choosing your bullseye target market to find a different specialty that won't require after hours call. Maybe you'll decide to just do new construction and just run all of the pipes before they put the drywall into the home.

I have a friend who is a physician who has avoided after hours issues by making his business model one that is a clinic only. He has no hospital affiliation or emergency numbers, so he doesn't ever worry about late night calls.

Thinking all of these things through in the beginning means you'll have fewer surprises later, both financially and emotionally. You may also find that you can stage your plan and some of your expenses. In the beginning, you may want to use a cell phone and forward all calls to that number outside of regular business hours. As business improves, you might consider an answering service so you don't need to take every call. Some afterhours calls are not really emergency calls and you'll find that they can be time consuming and annoying, particularly if you work from an office and don't have everything you need to answer questions about billing or scheduling.

Exercise 15

How many phone lines will you need? (don't forget a dedicated fax line)

Do you need a toll free number?

How will you handle after hours calls?

If you will have someone answering calls, have you made arrangements to have forwarding for these calls or will you have an emergency number? Who will that be?

Domain Name

You'll need a simple website with a professional email address. When choosing a domain name, it's alright if you can get your company name. If your company name is extremely long, you may think about a shortened version for your domain name.

It's even better if you can get a name that describes your business and your city, if you have a regional business. If you're a mortgage broker in Delray Beach, you might want it to be mortgagesdelray.com. When it's time to do Search Engine Optimization (SEO) for your business you'll thank me.

It's also important to own the .com suffix for your business. Buying .org or .net will cause you to be confused with whoever has that name and that may cost you business. When you buy your domain, I would suggest that you by the .org and .net domains of the same name. That is the best way you to control the name.

You can reserve your domain name at many different sites. The first consideration is how much they charge on an annual basis and you'll find they range from $10 to $43, depending on the company.

Some of these are:

> Godaddy.com
> Networksolutions.com
> Register.com

Thinking about how you might eventually get your website done will help you decide who to choose, since some of them offer templates for a fee so that you can design it yourself and get it up more quickly. This is not a perfect solution for your site. Although I can't guarantee this, I have been told that Google doesn't take sites on some of these templates seriously, and doesn't rank them well, if at all.

Your business email should be centered from your domain such as service@ mortgagesdelray.com . It shouldn't be a free email from yahoo or any of the others. In many cases, you can set up a mail box even before you get your website done, which will allow you the appearance of professionalism. If you want to be able to see your email on your phone, you can forward your email to a Gmail email, and you won't miss anything, yet when you respond, it will just state that it was send from your phone.

Exercise 16

Brainstorm domain names that contain your most important keywords in them. Be sure they are .com names. If you are a regional business, don't be afraid to include that in your keywords. I can't tell you whether it is better to have your city at the front of the keywords or at the end of the keywords. I only know that when I am googling for a product or service, I generally put in the keywords first followed by the city.

Go to http://www.godaddy.com to see if any of them are available. If you are a regional service professional, use your city or region name in your domain name. It will make it easier to get the domain, and it will help you be found.

Reserve the domain name and formulate an email name.

Website

This will not get you immediate clients, but in this day and age, your website can be more important than your physical business address. For that reason, I will tell you to get your website set up before you do anything else. It doesn't need to be a top of the line website, but it needs to be there with your basic information. You can do one of these yourself using a basic word press template. These are very easy to set up, and won't take you more than a couple of hours. As time goes on, you can change it, have it professionally done, add to it, etc.

If you decide to have someone else do your site, I suggest you go to http://99designs.com before going anywhere else. You can go onto their site, describe what you want done, tell them how much you want to spend, and you will get a preliminary design back before you hire anyone. The only caveat is that you will need to escrow your money so that they know you are really going to hire someone from that site to do your work. What's cool about it is that everyone can see everyone else's work, which inspires them to each do better than the last.

If you decide to do the first site yourself, here are a few web hosting companies that have readymade templates I have found easy to use:

www.1and.com
http://www.1and1.com

www.lunarpages.com
http://www.lunarpages.com

www.godaddy.com
http://www.godaddy.com

secure.hostgator.com
http://secure.hostgator.com

You want to have at least 5 pages on your site :

Home Page

This page should attract the attention of your visitors. You have about 6 seconds to grab their attention enough to keep them there. The best way to do that is to follow these guidelines:

- Have a powerful headline that will make them identify with you and say "yes, this is what I'm looking for". To do this, you want to specifically identify and state the problem that they need help solving. The best way to do this is to really think about who your customer is.

- Your subheading tells them that you can solve the problem. Tell them that it will be alright because you know the answer

- Your copy should tell them more about what your company can do and why. It can include your story about why you decided to help them solve this specific problem.

- Place a testimonial or two on this page to reinforce your credibility.

- Be sure your contact information is prominent on this and every page.

Contact Page

This is the second most important page because it gives them a means to contact you, and since you're on the net to be found, you want to give them as many ways as possible to easily reach you.

Your contact page should have your phone number and an email address at the very minimum. Putting a contact form on that page will demonstrate that you are professional and are eager to be contacted.

I don't actively promote putting your mailing address on there if you work out of your home. You will take the risk of having perspective clients and salespeople just show up on your doorstep, and if you are like most of us, that could be convenient or embarrassing.

Testimonials

This is vitally important on your website. I also call this a "referral page" because in effect, the people who have given you testimonials are actually referring you to the people who visit your site. Be sure that the testimonials are genuine. When possible, list their first and last names, their cities, and their websites.

As soon as you have testimonials, get them onto your site. Even better is if you can use http://www.freeconferencecall.com and have your happy clients call in and record their testimonials. Then you can put the audio on your website for the entire world to hear. Their enthusiasm and realness come through and you turn golden as they speak.

About Us

This is the place to tell your story. How did you come to start your company? Why did you start your company? What event or experience did you have that ignited your passion for what you can do for them?

This is a great place for your prospects to get to know you, your family, and your employees. It should tell them about your business, your interests, whatever organizations you're involved in, any awards you may have won, and anything else you want to brag about.

Lots of pictures can add to the value of this page. Please restrict your photos to business pictures. You might add pictures of your office or workshop, your employees, your products, or your company vehicles.

Services

This should be a list of all the unique services that you offer as well as your standard services. It's important to list both because this page gives them an overview of your company's strengths and may jog their memories about something that they wanted but that wasn't necessarily at the top of their minds at the moment. It may be one sale, or an addition to the one thing that they were already coming to you for.

Exercise 17

Decide whether you will do your own website or have someone else do it for you.

If you decide to have someone else do it for you, go to http://99designs.com or to http://www.odesk.com and put your site out for bids. List the result.

Spend some time thinking about what you want to put on your site. Look at other sites to see what appeals to you, but remember that this site is not about you, it is about your customers. List sites that you like and what you find appealing about them.

Gather photos, videos or audios to put on your site. List them here.

Write articles related to your industry to put on your site. List 5 here.
1.)

2.)

3.)

4.)

5.)

Your Logo – Recognition

Now that you know about who your customer is and what you will do for them, you can have a designer do a logo for you.

It should adequately represent who you are as a company and what you do.

There are a ton of designers out there who are all looking for work. I have had local designers do great work for me. In a situation where I felt the logo wasn't important, I went onto 99 Designs and put it out for bids. It's an interesting concept, and I must admit that the owner is a friend of mine. Basically, you go online, tell them what you want, how much you are willing to pay, put the money in escrow with them, and you will get so many design samples, it will amaze you. You can give them feedback and ask them to make changes, and then choose one that you like. If you don't like any of them, you don't have to take any of them and you can get your money back. I believe that they will encourage you to put it out for a second bid with different instructions, because they are concerned about having the designs stolen. Honestly it amazes me that people will do that, especially since these are people who will also be business owners and would never want to be treated that way.

When you are looking at designs, keep in mind that you want something that will translate well into black and white so that it can be seen by someone who prints out your letterhead or invoice in black and white. It shouldn't be too busy. Remember that you will pay for printing by the number of colors that you need to have printed. Try to keep it to two colors for best effect, lowest price, and easiest translation into black and white.

Business Cards

After you've compiled all of the above information, you're ready to have some business cards created. You should have your logo by now, since it doesn't take very long, but if you don't, and you are ready to go out and get business, make a small number without a logo. Having business cards will be important to prove that you are a serious business owner. If you email your proof to any of the major office supply stores, and probably some local office supply stores, they can print them in one day for a very small fee. Call your local office supply store to ask if they can provide this service and get their email information.

For your initial startup, if you have a small amount of talent, you can invest in Microsoft Publisher to design your cards. If you have some ability, this program will really be useful to you to help you design some basic propaganda to distribute, including brochures, fliers, postcards, and other mailing pieces.

Include the following information on your card: your name, your company name, title, phone number, address (if you have a separate business address), a brief description of what you do, and a tag line ("helping service professionals get more clients at higher fees" is an example of this.)

Your cards should be clean and professional. I've seen very elaborate business cards, and what I've learned about them is that as long as it has the basics, nothing else matters, unless your services are extremely high end. In that case, you should invest in the most expensive business cards there are. They set the tone for the service that you provide.

If networking will be a big part of your marketing, you may want to invest in a professional business card so you can make use of both sides of the card rather than making one side too busy.

From past experience, I believe that you should never give a business card to anyone unless they ask for it. Otherwise, it will probably end up either in the garbage, on the ground, or in the bottom of the washing machine within 24 hours.

Exercise 18

Think about the type of logo that will describe your company. What does it need to get across?

Call several logo designers or find someone online. Decide who you will work with for your logo design.

Decide whether to make your cards or to have someone else design them.

Whatever you decide to do, act on it now.

Resolve to have your business cards within five days and follow through.

Contact Management Software

This is so important to your success that I felt it needed to be included with the basics. Nothing is more important than keeping track of everyone that you meet. Little pieces of paper with names scribbled on them and loose business cards lying all over your desk, going through your pockets in the laundry and even yellow notepads, do not qualify as a contact management system.

You can do this manually if you feel you must, by using a notebook, but there are many drawbacks to doing this, and it's such an outdated way of doing business that it scares me to believe anyone would actually think this is acceptable.

You need contact software that will not only keep track of who your contacts are and how to find them, but one that will let you separate them into different categories so that if you want to mail to a specific group, they are all in one place and a minimum wage person can copy the names and addresses from one list onto whatever you're mailing them.

Some of them allow you to track not only your current clients, but you can track and plan how to follow up with potential clients, and keep records of what their situations are so that you can bring them closer to being clients without forgetting them.

There are several good ones. The leading one seems to be ACT!, and they make it for many different industries so that you'll have the appropriate categories (and because then they can charge you more for providing for your specific need). There are many others that will work. You will find some that are specific for your industry other than Act!, and many will be less expensive. An online search should bring up what you need by searching for "Contact Management Software" along with your industry.

Think about this: If you lose one potential client, how much will it cost you? If they had become a lifetime client, how much would THAT cost you? You now know the value of a good contact management system, and the importance of using it.

This organization can make or break your business. It's right up there with overcoming your natural desire to use the 5 pocket accounting system to track your income and expenses.

Exercise 19

What are your specific needs going to be?

Do you need email capabilities only?

How detailed do you want the contact information to be?

Some of your contacts will be different than others. How will you track them?

Do you want them to be tracked in separate lists?

Will you be able to access your contact list from anywhere?

Will your list be online, so you don't need to worry about losing it if your computer crashes, or will you need to be careful to back up your computer on a regular basis?

Accounting Software

This is the "F" word. The dreaded word. Financial stuff overwhelms many new business owners and they do their best to avoid even thinking about it, never mind doing it. I must admit that in the old days, before I knew better, I tried to avoid facing this information. Now I understand that this is my best friend.

For those of you who are just starting, I suggest that you first find an accountant that you feel comfortable with. Many of you will never feel comfortable with any accountant because your personalities are so different. It is okay. Find one who you believe will protect you.

I suggest that you use a version of Quickbooks that your accountant can access from his office. This will make your life much easier, and allow you to be able to at least pull out reports so you can see where you are financially. The reason I suggested that you get the accountant first is because not all accountants use this version of Quickbooks, and it will save you time and trouble if you don't need to run to the accountants office frequently.

Now I suggest that you have the accountant set up Quickbooks for you according to your needs. From this point you have two choices. I recommend that the accountant show you a couple of basic things:

- How to write invoices
- How to record deposits
- How to write checks
- How to check your balances

If this completely overwhelms you, find a part time bookkeeper. I know your accountant will tell you that you should just let him do the work, but there is no reason to pay CPA fees for simple tasks. When you are not feeling so overwhelmed, learn how to do those basic things that I mentioned above. You don't ever want to feel like an untrusted child in your own business who is not allowed to know what is going on.

You will also want to set up a financial dashboard so that you can keep an eye on your business on a monthly basis. Doing this will allow you to understand everything that is going on in your business without you even being there. The following information should be in your financial dashboard:

Total Sales
Total Cost of Goods
Total Expenses
Total Payroll
Net Profit

If you look at any of these, you will be able to know a lot about the business, provided that your business is using a cash accounting system. For instance, suppose you are an air conditioning company. If you have sold a lot of new systems last month, you would know by the cost of equipment. If your payroll was really high, but your cost of goods was low, you would know that you had a lot of service calls. If your expenses were really high, you would know to take a look at the full financials from the accountant to see why your expenses were higher than usual. If your income is high, you could look at your marketing to see if there was something specific that you had done to cause the increase. You could also look back and compare it to another time when you used the same marketing to see if this occurs each time that you do this marketing.

Working with a good accounting system will save you an incredible amount of money. It also prevents your employees from spending recklessly as you grow. Understand that this will be your best friend, and a valuable asset.

Exercise 20

Do some research to find an accountant. Ask other business owners for a referral. Find one that has a good understanding of the type of business you have.

Set up your bookkeeping software, and be sure that even if you won't be the one using it, you know how to access it and to find some of the basics.

Chapter 5

Getting Clients – Miracle Grow Touch Guideline Strategies

Marketing Basics

So what is marketing? Most people think that marketing is advertising. Actually, advertising is only one aspect of marketing.

Marketing is telling people who your business is and what it does in the simplest form. It's a way of disclosing your identity to the masses with the hope that the masses will want to get to know you. It is not a onetime event; it is a systematic way of life.

There are many different forms of marketing, using all of the different medias, such as the web, newspaper, public speaking, direct contact, etc. The important part is that you tell the public repeatedly who you are and what you do.

Marketing doesn't need to cost money, if you have more time than money, you can spend time. Where you start depends on your own preferences and abilities. You may be a great writer, or you may be a great speaker. Whatever you feel most comfortable with is where you should start.

Since it is a system, you need to develop your plan and, as Nike says, "Just Do It!"

Causes of Marketing Failure

What generally stops most business people from successfully marketing their product is one of four things;

- Fear
- Lack of Motivation
- Ignorance
- Poor Time Management

All of these things can be easily overcome just by making a few changes

Problem 1 – Fear

Fear of not knowing what to do, how to do it, and how to put it together. As simple as these things sound, unless you've learned the right way to market your business, you may think that you're better off to do nothing rather than do the wrong thing. I've heard so many professionals refer to a successful business owner and say "He's a natural salesman". In some cases it may be true, but in the majority of cases, it's just that they know what to say to whom, where to find them, and when.

The second fear is fear of rejection. No one wants to get that look that says "Don't make me tell you that I'm not interested" when you know that they now see you as the enemy because they are afraid that you will try to sell them something that they don't want.

Solution

You've already begun this part. Education can cure most fears. Reading this book and implementing some of the methods contained here will go a long way to help you increase your business in the next few months. Being considered a "natural salesman" is really a matter of confidence. Like the scarecrow in the Wizard of Oz, who thought he didn't have a brain, you have everything you need to be a great salesperson for your business already. You just need a little bit of information to nudge you forward, and you're already more than halfway there now.

If you use the one sentence method to describe what problem you solve, you won't ever have to sell anything. You will find that anyone who is interested will respond to your sentence with "How do you do that?" which allows you to tell them more. If they aren't interested, they won't ask and you won't get the rejection that you are afraid of. If they don't ask for more information, they are not prospective clients. It's a great way to locate your prospective clients and to weed out those who will never be clients.

Problem 2 - Motivation

Staying motivated is easier when you need to be accountable to someone else. It's just human nature. This can be particularly difficult when you are a solopreneur. Unless you have a really strong inner voice that keeps you going, it is difficult to convince yourself that you need to stay focused. It's much easier when you have a partner or even some employees to help keep you going and to have to report to. Accountability is a huge problem for many solopreneurs who may work alone without speaking to other people for much of the day. In some cases, these solopreneurs get to the point where they just don't want to speak with anyone.

Many business owners want to sit around and wait for the phone to ring. They get out of bed with no specific plan for their day, other than to answer the phone, or go on an appointment that is already scheduled. Consequently, it is easy to just coast through the day and justify it by thinking about what they did do, rather than what they should have done. They may have a list of things they know that they need to do for their marketing, but they don't ever get around to it. There is always something else they can do instead. They would rather read all of the junk mail on their desk, talk to people who will never bring them money, or fix a piece of equipment rather than make some calls or go out and network. They tell themselves that they need to be in the office just in case....

Solution

I always suggest finding a noncompeting business owner in the same position so you can force each other to be accountable to do what you need to do. There are many lateral business people who also have the same needs. Another suggestion is to find a mastermind group. This is better than a buddy because they may also give you some new ideas. If you don't have a buddy, hire a coach. A good coach can also help you formulate new ideas or look at things differently. It will be the best money that you spend in your business.

Schedule specific items to do every day. Even if you aren't going to a networking event, you can make some follow up calls or email new contacts each day. It's important to be involved in working on your business every day, rather than working in it. This means that each day you need to do something that will specifically result in furthering your business. These are not things that cost you money, but do take up about an hour of your time. At the end of the day, be sure that everything that you had scheduled is checked off your list. If it is an item that takes less than 15 minutes, stay and do it. If it is something that can't be completed today, carry it over to tomorrow's list. A caveat here – you will have to be sure to stay and do the entire list at some point. Otherwise it is too easy to just let the list grow. If you see that happening, be advised that you are endangering your business and you'll see the effect when your business goes down.

Problem 3 – Ignorance

They say that ignorance is bliss, and for those who don't understand how to run and build a business, this is especially true. This is the business owner who blames the universe because he isn't successful. It never occurs to him that there might be something that he doesn't know, although he will generally admit that there is one thing he doesn't like to do, and that is to sell.

Many people think that marketing is advertising, and therefore is as simple as deciding to run an ad. They let the advertising company design an ad for them based on a limited amount of information that they provide to the sales rep. Then believe that the ad that they get must be good because it was professionally done. They don't know whether it accurately represents them. This generally provides the business owner with another frustration because his ad never pulls in very much business, and he rants because he knows that he has wasted his hard earned money.

What he doesn't realize, is that his problem actually started long before this event. It started when he set up his business and had his logo, brochures, and all of his other setup items designed without benefit of a simple business plan. He doesn't see that to others he is actually invisible, because he has nothing out of the ordinary or remarkable to offer.

The graph for this business is generally fairly flat. He starts his business and makes barely enough to stay alive, and it never gets better. His advertising is as unfocused as his business, and he can throw all the money he has into advertising, but it will be completely ineffective. He will blame the media he is using to advertise in, and will never admit that the problem might be internal. He just doesn't know any better.

If he is lucky, he will still manage to stay in business, but in some cases, he will not be this lucky. This is the M.O. of a business that should and could have stayed in business. This is the "If Only" business. If only he had gotten some basic marketing and management help, he would have been a success. He was unaware that he could change this because he didn't know he needed help. If he did figure out that he needed help, he didn't know where to look for it, and he was too afraid to ask another business owner for help.

Solution

As you've already learned, if you try to appeal to everyone, you appeal to no one. If you don't understand the basics of marketing, you can't possible develop effective ads. Advertising only works when you have good marketing in place. It is what you can do once you've decided what your marketing will focus on.

In order to advertise to your best advantage, you need to know your Bullseye target market. Once you do that, you can just tell them what you do and they will be able to design your ad simply, at less cost, and in less time than it would take otherwise.

Good marketing requires good presence, distinctive features, and positive energy.

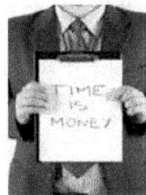

Poor Time Management

Poor time management and neglecting to just schedule time to market your business are a problem for service professionals who have been in business for a while. Much of this comes from wanting to believe that after you've been in business for a while, you shouldn't have to market your business. You should just miraculously have enough clients forever. Although this can happen eventually if you're an expert at what you do, you probably don't want to count on it for quite some time. The prevailing attitude among most service professionals is that they will fit it in when they don't have anything else to do. They can generally find something else to do, rather than marketing, and find their business "stuck" at a specific level.

They show a pattern of financials that looks like a rollercoaster. It starts to rise, then falls again. Then it rises, to about the same level, but falls again. The reason this happens is generally because they get to a point of business loss, where they realize that they need to go out and find some business. These business owners are completely inconsistent about their marketing, because they would rather have appointments than pay attention to their marketing, so at times when they get busy, they are relieved to be able to claim to not have time to market. Sooner or later, they run out of clients, and need to go out and find new ones.

This is the biggest problem I find with owners who are good at what they do. They want to go on appointments and do what they like doing. The problem is that they are so busy working in their business, that they don't have time to work on their business and they will never be able to grow past their current level. These are the ones who just want to fill in the times that aren't busy. They don't understand that business doesn't work that way.

Solution

Before you schedule clients for the week, schedule your marketing time. If there are specific events that you do well, schedule those first, and consider them as important as client time. If you know you have copy to write, calls to make, etc., be sure to schedule those. DO NOT cut out your marketing time to take care of a client or go to a doctor's appointment. You must make it a priority.

The only real answer is to hire someone to work for you. I know what you are thinking as you read this. I hear it all the time. They always tell me that they can't afford to hire someone. The truth is that they can't afford not to hire someone. This is especially true in the current environment.

So think about these options. It is very easy, in many businesses, to do one of two things. First, you can hire someone who will work on commission only who will go out and help you to get business. It will take some time to train them, but can be very worthwhile. Second, you can hire someone on a part time basis to service your clients. They get paid either for a small number of hours, or only for what they do. In other words, they will be doing piece work. They would get a straight fee per client call. You can train them while you are not excessively busy. This will free up some time for you to go out and do some marketing to help you build more business and pay for your new hire. Then, as you get busier, this person can work more hours, freeing you up to do more for your business. It also puts you in a position of coming in only for the tough stuff that your service person can't handle it.

One side effect is that you will be so much more aware of building your business, that when you do go out on a client call it changes the way you handle those calls. You'll find yourself asking the client for referrals, or other professionals who might help you to get more business. The truth is that the more you work on your business, the more you will _want_ to work on your business. You will work faster on the service call, so you can get on to more important things. In many cases, you'll eventually find that you go on very few service calls. In fact you may resent having to go out on appointments.

Changing A Habit

You've read the four problems that affect most business owners when it comes to marketing. This is one area where you will need to push yourself for the sake of your business, unless you have a partner. For your own success, you need to be able to successfully market your business.

Everyone who reads this book will resolve to overcome their issue, and will make an attempt to change what they do. Yet only about 4% of the people who are reading this book will actually succeed. This happens because they start working toward solving the problem, but they get distracted and never finish.

It takes three months to change a habit. It doesn't become natural until then. That means that you need to really look at this, commit to it, and schedule it. If you say you are going to do something but you don't schedule it, then it won't happen. That darned human nature takes over and lets us backslide.

The Cost of Acquiring a Client

You've heard me mention the cost of acquiring new clients. Let's talk about that a little more in detail. In any marketing, there is a cost. If you are just beginning your business, or if your time is not fully booked, then it is better to use your time to build your business rather than spending a great deal of money on advertising. This is one of those things that you will need to monitor closely, and be sure that you aren't lying to yourself.

When you are doing any marketing, it is important to know what the costs are to your company. There is a very simple formula to use to determine what that cost is. Cost of your time + cost of promotion + cost of materials = Total Cost. Then take the Total Cost and divide it by the number of new clients that you received as a result of what you did. The number of clients you received would be your Client Cost. The formula will look like this:

$CT + CP + CM = TC$

$$\frac{TC}{NC} = CC$$

For example, if you ran a newspaper ad that cost a total of $400, and 2 hours of your time at $100 per hour for follow up phone calls, and that told readers to call for a free report that cost you $3 including postage, and the entire thing netted you 6 new clients, you can calculate by using all of the above numbers this way:

$$\$200 + \$400 + \$3 = \$603$$
$$\frac{\$603}{6} = \$100.50 \text{ per new client}$$

The cost of your new client is $100.50.

How much is this new client actually worth to you?

What can you expect an average client to pay you the first time he uses your service? Will he need to use your service more than once?

You may have a service that the client will use just once. If that is the case, you will need to be sure that the fee will be a total of the Cost of Acquisition + Total Rate based on your hourly fee. If you are making just enough to cover the new client cost, but you aren't making enough to pay you for your service, you can't make a living.

If your service is one that will be repeated, and you can make repeated money on this client, then I suggest that your average fee needs to be 1.5 times the cost of a new client, particularly if you are new in business. The reason is that if you are new in business and the majority of clients are coming from your advertising, you won't make enough money to stay in business. You can't just get your cost back because that doesn't give you any income.

I know that the SBA tells you that if you have a new business, you should expect to lose money for the first three years, but I find that to be completely ridiculous. Why would you go into business to lose money? I suppose that may be true for larger small businesses, but when you are operating at "boutique size", which is where all of my clients start, you aren't being given money through grants or loans to allow you to lose money. My clients are generally investing their own hard earned dollars, and losing money for a long period of time is just not an option!

Caution - Marketing Exposure Overload

It is important to remember that you can have a challenge when it comes to marketing. Every day we are bombarded with marketing messages every way we turn. You are not even conscious of most of them. That's why it is so important to discover your identity.

As you plan your marketing strategy, you need to keep in mind that statistics show that most people are being exposed to 5000 marketing messages every day. It is marketing exposure overload!

The challenge is to push your message to the forefront of these messages and make your Bullseye Market remember you. That may seem overwhelming, but in truth, it is easier to impress people than you think because you will stand out if your message is clear and distinctive. That is why, if you are truly appealing to your Bullseye Market, and they need you at that time, you'll have their interest within 10 seconds.

Statistics show that when you are marketing, there will be 3% that will need you at that time. There will be another 7% who is thinking about what you have to offer, and another 20% who will need you sometime in the future. Thirty percent will think about using you in the future even though they never considered that they would, and another 30% will never use you.

If you are marketing to them at a time when they don't need your service, you must understand that it will take time for them to remember you and buy your service. Statistics claim that in the 1970s it took four exposures to your message before they would buy. In the 1990s it was 7 to 10 exposures. Now the estimates are 11 to 14 exposures before the public will remember you. That means that you need to do a lot of marketing to build your business so that when they are looking for your service, they will remember you and go directly to you.

That's why I came up with the concept of the Miracle Grow Touch Guidelines. These will help you delineate your marketing methods and remind you that it will take repeated exposure to your potential market before they remember you and trust you enough to buy your product. In some cases it is possible to speed up the process with personal contact. Since people learn using different senses, when someone meets you, they will not only see your message, they can hear you talk about yourself and your business and shake your hand.

Exercise 21

Which of the four marketing problems is the one that you have the most trouble with?

What will you do to overcome it?

Take one step toward fixing this problem today. Schedule the balance of the cure on your calendar to be done during the next 90 days.

Trust Building Systems

As mentioned before, your potential customers may not buy immediately. I'm sure that you don't want to accept that your business will experience this, but most people do business with businesses that they trust. There are exceptions to this rule, but whenever possible, this is the way most intelligent people like to make decisions.

Until you build trust and credibility you will have issues with both a lack of clients and refund requests from those that you do have. You really have to convince the consumer that you are not going to hurt them. It used to be that you called whoever was in your community who did what you needed. Now communities are too large. It's sad that this has happened in our country. You don't know your neighbors anymore. There is anonymity in our country that didn't exist 50 years ago.

I recently read a letter from a man named Scott Heiferman, who is the CEO of meetup.com. It was on the tenth anniversary of 9/11, and he talked about the fact that the reason his company was born was because of 9/11. He said that he lives in New York, and didn't know any of his neighbors until that day. He was so excited about interacting with great people that he had never before met, that he put up a website that would help people meet each other in person to talk and help each other.

I grew up in a time when you trusted the local professional because you knew that he was worried about his reputation so he always gave you more value than you expected. Then big cities became prevalent. People stopped socializing the way they used to. We no longer sit on our front porches and talk to the neighbors. We no longer know all of our neighbors.

The way service professionals do business has also changed. It used to be that a service person knew that he had to do a good job or risk losing his reputation. Now, if someone doesn't do a good job, they can change the name of their company and do it all again and get clients who he hasn't dealt with yet. When he runs out of a sufficient number of people in that city, he can always move to another city and start all over again.

We've all had experience with trust in our personal relationships during the course of our lives, starting with building trust with our parents when we were growing up. We built friendships in school and at other times.

For these reasons, we know that trust doesn't happen overnight. There are things that we can do to speed the process, as long as we acknowledge that there is a process to earning trust, and it doesn't happen on its own. It needs our personal attention.

The Trust Timeline

So now instead of instant trust (also known as trusting until you can't trust) there is a trust time line. It used to be described in the past as the number of times someone needed to be exposed to your message before they remembered it. Now it is much more than that. It is the number of times they are exposed to you and your message before they believe it. Your messages to them must convey your business character before they will buy, and they must feel that your character is worthy of their trust. This is much more the issue than being memorable. Remembering you is only one part of the equation now. Earning trust is the other part.

It will take repeated messages of any kind just to get them to remember you. Some of these messages will be in person. Some will not. Impersonal media will help them remember you, but those messages won't build trust. Personal meetings will help you to earn their trust. It is a slower progression than advertising, but it is nonnegotiable when you're building your business.

The trust time line will be different for everyone, depending on the general personality of your potential client and their life experiences. Some will trust you more easily. Others will take much longer.

Imagine that in your business, when you were just starting, you hired an attorney to set up your company. Lawyers generally gain trust easier than many professionals when it comes to believing them. They may not always have your trust in regards to billing, but they do when it comes to advice. So you set up your business the way he suggested, and paid him $5000, and later found out that this entity was not at all what you needed and you then had to pay someone else to do it all over. You would be more leery the second time, and would probably want to interview a few attorneys before you hired another one. You might ask for references, or you might only go to someone who has been recommended by another business person.

This is just a mild example. There are outright unscrupulous "professionals" out there. It's been my experience that this happens more frequently when they haven't had to work to earn their license and don't fully appreciate their responsibility to the public. These people have stolen money from consumers on more than one occasion, and even if it hasn't happened to you, chances are it's happened to someone you know.

When you think about all of that, you can understand the reluctance that most people have to hiring you until they have had several encounters with you and get to know you better.

In whatever way these encounters are accomplished, it generally takes seven to twelve of these "touches" for a potential client to trust you. A "touch" is any form of positive contact. Sometimes it only takes seven touches, especially if you are using good strategies, but sometimes it takes longer, particularly if your message is not definitive enough or you don't appear sincere.

"Touch" is really just such a nice word, but maybe caress would be even better, because you really want to stroke your clients so they will relax and lean toward you instead of holding themselves back. If you watch their body language, you can see it happen.

Have you ever watched the family pet? When you pet them, they always start to lean in toward you, because you make them feel good. You want to make your clients feel good also. You do that by giving them something to help them – free information works really well. This is specific reassurance that tells them that you can help them, that you know what you are talking about, and that you are willing to demonstrate it and help them by educating them.

Free information is a vitally important part of your marketing plan because it helps to build trust and credibility. By giving them some of your knowledge, it shows them that you are the expert in your field. Everyone wants to work with an expert. Why? They know that they aren't wasting their money, and that what they receive from you will be the best there is. They know they will get their money's worth.

The Miracle Grow Touches also show them that you are not a fly by night, in it to make a buck and off you go. When my daughter was young, she had a Disney book about a race between Goofy and Mickey. Goofy had an old jalopy that kept the same pace all the time. Mickey had a fast car and stopped several times for treats along the way. To Mickey's great surprise, slow and steady Goofy won the race. The story always made me laugh because Goofy's mantra all the way through was "Slow and steady, steady and slow, that's the way we always go". Your mantra should be the same for your marketing plan. Building trust needs to be done gently and honestly.

Your marketing plan needs to incorporate many of the Miracle Grow Touches because you are demonstrating that you care about your business and you like what you're doing enough to keep doing things to work on it.

It also demonstrates to the public that you've thought your business through and feel that you can do more for them and take better care of things that matter to them than your competitor can.

Building on Initial Trust

When someone finally decides to try you, they do so cautiously. That means that it is now in your hands to build this relationship. You now have to show them that you are worthy of their trust. How do you do this?

First, you must do what you say you will do. That means that you don't take on a task that you aren't equipped to do. Sometimes we take on something because we need the money and we think that it can't be that hard to figure out. Are you sure about that?

Second, you must do it in the time you say you will do it. Showing up late or putting someone off really offends someone who needs to have something completed. Time is money for everyone these days, and if they find themselves calling you repeatedly, they will not be raving fans. Even worse is when you start something and it takes you forever to get it done.

This can happen when you take on something that you thought you could figure out and it takes you longer to do because you are making it up as you go along.

Third, you must do it for the amount that you said you would do it. This is a really big problem for many businesses because there are variables that can't be controlled, such as what is inside what you can see. This is a problem for contractors, and many repairmen. The only way to handle this issue is to have a very frank conversation with the client. For instance, I have a very complex system of crowns and bridges in my mouth. Recently I had to change dentists because my dentist retired. I had a problem with a bridge that became loose. The new dentist carefully explained that although there were some things that he could see, there was a lot under that bridge that he couldn't see until he got the crown off. So he prepared me for what he felt would be worse case. I asked what would happen if the problem was bigger. He explained that he thought I might not even need what he said I would need, but if it did, he would eat the balance (so to speak). He backed up his theory with good believable facts and I trusted that he knew what he was talking about. The fee was huge, but after I picked my jaw up off the floor, and since I knew what the maximum amount would be, I agreed to let him do the work. He cemented my decision by giving me a guarantee that it would be perfect or I didn't have to pay him.

Three Things People Believe About Experts

When you talk about your business knowledgeably, and give away some free information, you show your expertise.

* Almost all experts are very busy people, whether they are serving clients or learning new things that they are curious about. That means they will do what you need done quickly and efficiently so that they can go on to other things.

* The second belief is that experts love what they do. If you love what you do, you do it well because it makes you feel good. Pride in workmanship is a rare commodity, and if you exhibit it, you'll have customers for life. You also don't mind doing some extra things when you love what you do, so your customers will directly benefit.

- The third belief is that if you are the expert, there is nothing that you don't know about your area. People worry that they will hire someone only to discover later, that they don't know what they need to know to complete the job. If that happens, it will then take a long time to complete the job, because the professional is learning while he's on the job, and probably charging you for it. In some cases, the professional will never be able to finish, because he just can't figure it out. This is everyone's worst nightmare and it happens frequently.

So you can see why it may take time for them to trust you. Some things can't be rushed. This is one of them.

Return Clients Reduce Marketing Costs

It takes time to build trust in business just as it would in any long term relationship. Let's be honest. That's what you're building here – a long term relationship. Here's why.

First, they need to trust you enough to at least sample your work. You may find that clients will dip their toe in the water before they dive in. If you prove yourself capable and trustworthy they will remember you the next time and may be a little braver about how much they spend with you then.

Second, the initial cost in time and money of attaining a client can be very high. Certainly as you are doing your marketing you will appreciate this even more. It can take months to get someone to trust you enough to use your services. When that finally happens, you'll want to keep them as a client, because the second time they buy your service, it doesn't cost you as much. Even though it may not have cost you money to get that customer, it has cost you time. Your time has a cost. For you, time is money, and by now, you should know how much your time is worth, so you can calculate the cost of a new client.

As an example, if you invest even an hour of your time to get one client, which is probably a lot less than you will actually invest, and you are charging $100 per hour, that customer cost you $100.

As you get clients, there may be some costs associated with keeping in touch with them, either in mailing costs or your small amount of time on the phone or in person, but the ground rules are set. They understand that you do what you say when you say you'll do it for the amount that you tell them it will cost. They know that if they ask you to do something that you aren't knowledgeable about, that you will recommend someone else. I believe that it is your responsibility to help them find someone who can help them. You understand that if you do what you say, and say no if they ask you to do what you can't, they will respect you and won't argue about whatever you charge them as long as they know what that will be. In many cases, they won't even ask how much it will cost after you earn their trust. This makes them more valuable than a new client.

This is why we spend time using the Miracle Grow Touch Guidelines to market a business and make Customers for Life. Over a long span of time, if you really make your clients love you, and if your business is geared to repeat business, you may not need to do as much marketing, which is exactly what you really wanted all along.

Exercise 22

Are you trustworthy? Do you do what you say you will do in the time you say you will do it under the conditions that you say you will do it?

What is your area of expertise?

Can you educate your market about aspects of what you do so they feel they are getting value? How?

How long does it currently take for someone to trust you?

What can you do to shorten that time?

Miracle Grow Touch Choices

Now you can understand the title that has been given to this practice. It takes several "touches" before your bullseye client will buy from you. Oh sure, some will jump right in and become a customer sooner. Some may never become customers. You will not accept others because they aren't ideal for you.

This leads us to talk about how to "touch" your prospects to get their attention and their trust sooner. This will be done by appealing to the primary sense of the person you are courting.

Building Instant Rapport

All people have a primary sense that they respond to and so need to be "touched" differently in order to learn and absorb what is presented to them. They may not always use the same sense to learn, but they do have a preference. By relating to them through their primary sense, they will not only learn better, but they will trust you sooner if you speak their language.

Although there are five senses, or modalities, for these purposes we will only talk about three, because these are the ones that affecting learning.

Visual

This refers to what people can see, which sounds simple enough, except that this has now been broken down into two separate groups. The first is as you would imagine, what people see when their eyes are open. This helps them to form mental pictures and to put things into perspective.

The second visual group is that group that feels the need to read. They have to read about everything, and they learn best by reading instructions.

Auditory

Auditory learners are those who learn by listening. They will never want to read, they will listen to books on tape. They are good at jobs that require that they be on the phone, such as customer service people, consultants, psychologists, etc.

Kinesthetic

Kinesthetic learners learn best by touching. Many of these people are sculpters, auto mechanics, welders, bakers, etc.

Building A Connection

The only way you will connect with people is in the manner which allows them to learn best. For that reason, it's beneficial to appeal to your potential customers in several different ways so that you find ways to relate to them. We will discuss these more in detail in the next section.

Miracle Grow Modalities

These senses are also known as modalities and when used properly and at the appropriate time, will help you to accomplish your goal of getting new clients and building your business.

Auditory

These can be any of the following:
Live Presentations
Taped Recordings

Teleclasses
Podcasts
Networking
Referrals
Radio Commercials/Audio Ads
Cold Calls
Phone Calls

Visual

Business Cards
Direct Mail
Written Reports
Videos/DVDs
Print Ads
Books
Pamphlets
Pictures
TV Commercials
Websites
Webinars
　　　　Press Release
　　　　Articles
　　　　Books

Kinesthetic

Promotional Items
Books
Food Items
Anything that can be touched, including a handshake

Many of these will fit into more than one modality category, because you can appeal to more than one sense at a time. It does not count as more than one touch each time.

How To Know What Sense To Use For Specific Clients

Knowing how to convince a specific person to trust you may be very important, particularly if you have really wanted to work for someone but haven't been able to reach a trust relationship with them. Sometimes just a little tweak can change your history with them. And anyone can do this.

If you are staring across your room at someone who is there with you and trying to figure it out, I'll make this very easy for you.

The first and easiest way is to ask them a question and listen to their answer. The way that they answer the question will tell you how they relate to the world.

You can ask them almost anything as long as it is not a yes or no question. Suppose you ask them to tell you about a problem they are having. They tell you about the problem, and they will usually tell you what their perception of the problem was. They will do this by saying any of these:

I saw myself...   Anytime that you hear a verb that refers to vision, you will know that you have a visual learner. This would also include the verb "imagine" because that generally refers to a vision.

I heard this noise... Noises can be very traumatic for some people and it is not because their ears are sensitive, but because they are auditory learners who have their hearing fine -tuned. It's best to not talk to them when there are a lot of loud noises because they are listening to a lot of things at the same time.

I felt myself... They will describe the weather, meaning whether it was hot or cold, the feel of fabrics, they will notice of someone has a cold handshake.

There will be synonyms for any of these verbs, but I'm sure that you get the idea. They will describe everything by using their primary sense.

Let's imagine that you are meeting someone for the first time. Suppose that you haven't been able to ask a question because he is speaking to someone else. You only need to listen to what he is saying. There are always language clues. He may talk about it being too hot or too cold, or talk about what he saw when he was coming in, or about an interview that he heard on the radio. That is a great beginning point.

Now let's suppose that you haven't had the opportunity to listen to him. All you can do is go by their body language. Maybe you see them across the room and you want to speak to them, but you know that he is very popular or very important and you may only have ten seconds to appeal to him when you finally get to speak to him.

Watch him across the room. If he is visual, you will see that he is using his hands to describe something to someone. The visual learner does that because he can see it in his mind. He is trying to recreate it for the person he is talking to. He doesn't want to hear anything. All that matters to him is what he can see.

If the person is auditory, you may see him close his eyes while he is listening. The auditory learner does this because he can absorb the information better with fewer distractions. He believes that he can say something to someone and that's all they need. He never sees the need for anything in writing because he'll probably never read it anyway.

If you see someone frequently touching the people that person is talking to, he is kinesthetic. If someone shows a kinesthetic person a statue, he will take it and run his hands over it. It makes it real to him. Kinesthetic people often feel unloved if they don't have physical human contact of some sort. A phone call won't do for them.

I am very auditory. I learn by listening. It is very difficult for me to read anything online. I love books on tape. My secondary sense is kinesthetic. I need to print it and hold it in my hand in order to absorb it. I could care less about what I see because I won't remember it later.

For the record, statistically the majority of people, 70%, are visual, so if you need to appeal to any one sense, that's a great starting place.

If you respond to people using their primary sense, it will build trust between you more quickly, because their perception is that you understand them. For example, try saying the following:

How did you see yourself resolving...?
What did he say when you told him....
How did you feel about......?
What was it like.....

Starting at this level will make your client want to spend more time talking to you. They will feel a kinship with you although they won't understand why. With just this one little "party trick", you'll gain more insight into whom he is.

One additional piece of information, although everyone has a primary sense, they also have a strong secondary sense. You have two chances that you'll hit either the primary sense or the secondary sense, but aiming for the primary sense is more powerful. In some cases, when it is not possible for them to use their primary sense, they will automatically use their secondary sense.

Exercise 23

Practice your listening and observation skills with people you already know. List some observations here

Determine what their primary and secondary senses are. You will see that in some people this will sometimes change in different situations. That's okay. Our interest is in first encounters with people in specific situations. List your results here.

Practice responding to them in their own modality. After you do this for a while it will become second nature. What have you discovered about other people?

Miracle Grow Touches

Okay. Now we've got the basic setup done. It's time to move on to how and when to use each one of them. There are unlimited numbers of things you can put in your marketing plan to perform these "touches", but there are a limited number of categories that you will use. Some of these will overlap, but we will discuss them where they are most appropriate.

1.) Networking/Referrals – this is always number one on my list because it is either very low cost or absolutely free
2.) Education/Information – always necessary and used in many forms throughout all of these touches
3.) Give Aways
4.) Demonstration
5.) Direct Contact
6.) Indirect Contact
7.) Publicity
8.) Keeping in Touch

Miracle Grow Touch Fine Points

Once you know what the choices and modalities are, you can start to use the above miracle grow strategies or develop new strategies to use in your marketing plan. The possibilities are endless, so we will try to give you some strategies based on what you need to accomplish. Your marketing plan should combine as many of these as you can comfortably and dependably do. I suggest that you start slowly and add as you master each one.

Monitor your results with each touch strategy so that you can fine tune it to get the most bang for your buck – in this case, the most clients in the least amount of time, because your time is worth money!

You'll need to keep a diary of your miracle grow touches rather than just winging it. You may remember a particular event as a negative experience, but if you met 25 people, reaffirmed relationships with 3, and got 6 new leads, it was a successful strategy and you need to repeat it again to see if you can keep building in the same way. You'll find distinctive patterns of what works and what doesn't. What you need to remember is that you still need to use as many different strategies as you can. You never know when something great will come to the front and surpass anything you've done before.

Keep in mind that you can only use one strategy per touch. In other words, if you meet someone and give them your business card, that is one touch. Each touch has to be performed independently, and some are more effective than others and may be more effective at specific times.

For example, if you send out a direct mail piece to people you've never met, although that is a touch, it will not be effective if they have never connected with you before. If you met these people the week before and then sent them a note, then it is an excellent second touch.

You'll have to use some common sense and think things through. What would make you want to hire a particular company? Be honest about this.

Using Your Strengths/Fixing or Avoiding Your Weaknesses

Understand your strengths and weaknesses before you make your marketing plan. What are you good at? What needs some improvement? There may be some areas where you need help. If that's the case, either find someone else who can do what needs to be done for you, or find a way to improve in that area.

Some things you just must do yourself, even if it is not something that you are currently good at doing. Although you can hire someone to go to networking events (or have your spouse or assistant do it) , it's better if you go to these events yourself. People want to know who they are trusting and who they are giving their money to, and personal meetings are a critical aspect of presenting your company properly. Think about how you feel when you know the owner of the company. Doesn't it make you feel more confident? It is the same when your clients know you. They know where the ultimate responsibility for their satisfaction rests.

Sometimes you may have personal physical issues that you'll want to correct. I've met business owners who are embarrassed about their teeth, their sagging jowls, their weight, etc. Those things can be fixed. If these kinds of things are affecting your ability to perform, don't hesitate to work on them. Do it now!

If there are things in your life or your background that can't be changed, deal with them honestly and go on. In this case I mean something that is beyond your control. I know a business owner whose son committed a horrible crime! For some people, that translated to the fact that the father must have taught him that those kinds of thing were okay. He dealt with it by apologizing to the community on behalf of his son, and explaining that if he did anything wrong as a father, it was probably that he had worked too much when his son was growing up. He suggested that everyone else learn from his mistake and spend more time with their own children. It was done sincerely, and earned him respect from more people than had ever even thought about him before. The community came together to hold this man up and he was able to go on with his business. Had he not talked about it, in all likelihood he would have lost a lot of business.

There are people who are just so uncomfortable in crowds or with new people that they really feel that they can't go out and meet new people, especially if they are in a large group. If that sounds like you, and you try it after you have your identity solidified, then you may need a partner. Sometimes known as the "Front Man" because that's where he appears – out front. He should be a principal in the company so he can honestly state that he is an owner. They don't need to be a majority owner. They can own a small percentage. This man/woman is worth their weight in gold. This person will be responsible for bringing in new business, which is what you need to make your business grow. I do suggest, however, that if you can work through this and get out there yourself, it will be worth it in the long run. This can't be avoided or ignored. If you aren't out networking, except for a few rare companies, you won't be able to really be successful.

If you are not a good writer, then hire one! It's simple to find plenty of people to fill the background roles. They can be hired at very reasonable fees at odesk.com or elance.com. These are freelance people who want to make money. You might also have or hire an employee who can write for you. If so, put them to good use!

One thing you do need to master is the art of the handshake. In my father's day, everything was done on a handshake, and a weak handshake made people very nervous. They believed that if you had a weak handshake then your character was also weak, and maybe you were lying. Your handshake should be firm, but not so hard that you squeeze the blood out of their fingers. If you take someone's hand and it feels frail, be careful to not squeeze too hard. I have seen the double handshake where they shake your hand and then cover your hand with their other hand. This has other connotations and should never be used unless you are interested in friendship or more. It is not a business handshake.

Be careful if you decide to give away promotional items. Try to be sure that they are appropriate and of the proper quality for what you want to accomplish. If you are a home builder, don't give them something that will fall apart before they get home. It might send a message that your houses aren't well built either.

Exercise 24

What do you need to change about yourself?

Do your own self-assessment. Be honest. List below your strengths and weaknesses.

How will you strengthen your weak spots?

Find some contractors who cover your weak areas. List them here

Chapter 6

The Most Important Miracle Grow Touch Methods

This list is only limited by your imagination. For that reason, I will name as many as I can think of. You can use these, or variations that you find to meet your needs. Everyone has different situations and purposes, so just because it isn't on my list doesn't mean that it isn't a viable strategy. As a matter of fact, if you come up with a strategy that I haven't listed and you're wondering whether it will work, please email me and share it at luann@successfanatic.com I'm always open to hearing about new strategies, and would love to expand this list.

You'll want to divide your contacts into four groups:

1. Direct Business Prospects
2. Referral Prospects
3. Business Providers
4. Others

The first two groups are vitally important to your success, and you want to have an equal mixture of both of those. The third group is important to keeping your business going easily, so weigh these carefully. The fourth group may move into one of the other groups at some point in time, so don't discard them.

Direct Business Prospects are those that you will directly do business with. These are potential clients who may need your services sometime in the future. You will divide these into different degrees of prospects, depending on their urgency. This is the 20% of a market that are interested in what you have to offer

Referral Prospects are those who will not become clients, but have definite connections with people who may want to become your clients. Some of these are people who will be in your power group. Your power group is a group of people who tend to be involved with people who could need your services. For example, attorneys, CPA's, media designers, and I.T. people will all work with new businesses. Therefore, whichever one sees them first can refer this client to other business people in your group. Another example would be a massage therapist, an acupuncturist, a chiropractor, and an alternative medical doctor would be another power group.

Business Providers are people who you need for your business to help you to keep your business running. This would include an I.T. professional, a printer, an attorney, etc.

Others are those who you have met who really don't fit into the above categories, although that is subject to change at any time. These are the ones who will get the least attention from you, unless they do something to cause a change in their status.

Networking

This is probably the fastest way to build a new business. Personal appearances at social or business events will help you make great connections in your community, whether it is online or off line.

Building Instant Rapport When Networking

Before I talk about specific networking events, I'd like to talk about an important aspect of relating to the people that you'll meet at these events. It is a technique which you can use and it is so appropriate to this area that I feel it must be included and discussed now..

One of the things that a good salesperson knows about is the value of modeling. Modeling is a method of finding a gesture or a quality that is used by the person you are speaking to and doing something similar. You don't want to do exactly what the other person is doing. That is known as mirroring and can be offensive to the other person if they catch on to what you are doing.

There are many ways to do this. These are just some:

a tilt of the head
a way of crossing your legs
a phrase that they use
the timbre of their voice
the speed of their voice
a hand gesture
their breathing
the way they sit or stand
a facial expression

I once had a client who was a slow talker. We couldn't see eye to eye on almost anything. This was before I understood the value of only working with my ideal clients. Even at that, in many ways she was an ideal client, but on this one issue we didn't agree and seemed to be at a stalemate. I thought I would have to sever the relationship.

One day, I decided to try to talk to her at the same pace she spoke. We instantly got along. What is really interesting is that after that, whenever I spoke to her I spoke normally and it was still okay! The reason for the permanent change was that she bonded with me in that ten minute slow talking phone call.

You can do the same thing by just matching their breathing. If you happen to be meeting with them in a quiet room, and their breathing is very relaxed, it is easy to match it. If they have a certain way of siting, sit similarly.

The possibilities in this area are endless. If you notice that they're quirky about something, and it's something you can relate to with them without insulting them, you should use this technique. Don't imitate them exactly because then they feel that you're making fun of them, but just casually do what they do. You'll be surprised at how it builds the bond between you.

Exercise 25

Observe people that you already know. Find mannerisms and habits that are unique to them. List them here.

Now slightly imitate their mannerisms and write down the results here.

When you are in public, be a people watcher. See what they do that you find interesting and that could be easily modeled. Practice modeling them to see if they begin to smile at you! List your successes here.

Personal Networking Opportunities

So where do you find networking opportunities? If your business is local, start with

Chamber of Commerce
BNI
local charities and organizations
trade organizations

It is easy to go and visit any of these groups by making an appointment ahead of time. If you go online to their websites, you will be able to contact them for information. Find out as much as possible about the group before you go to one of their gatherings, and take plenty of business cards.

Aside from structured networking events, you should keep in mind that any time you walk out of your house, you have an opportunity to network. Whether you are in the park or at the grocery store, you will have opportunities. For that reason, you need to be aware of how you present yourself at all times. People are aware of whom they are standing or sitting next to, and you only get one chance to make a good impression. For business purposes, you are working all the time. Therefore, you should always wear a name tag with your company name and your name, and clothes with the name of your company embroidered or printed on the pocket area.

Because you are working all the time, you also need to be aware of your behavior. Being a jerk will not increase your business. I also believe that you should have your business name on your car. It is okay to have a magnetic sign that you can take off if you are on your own time. I say that because, once again, you must be careful to realize that if you have your business delineated on your vehicle, then run someone off the road, it won't help your business.

I had a friend in my town who was an attorney. In his younger days he liked to raise a little Cain sometimes, but he was aware that he was well known everywhere in town. Periodically he would go out of town to just relax and stop being "on". He referred to this as "being at an away game". The fans (or the opposition) weren't watching.

Besides being involved with the Chamber, BNI, and local charities and organizations, you can go online to http://www.Meetup.com to find more opportunities for networking in your area. More and more groups are being formed all the time, so check this site from time to time.

In addition, do a Google search to find other websites that may have events that would be helpful. Where I live we have an art association that has a once a month art walk. This is a great place to connect with other people, and if you love art, it's just a great place to be. You can join a sports team or any type of hobby club that appeals to you. Doing what you genuinely love is a great way for prospective clients to learn more about you. Become involved in your child's school or after school activities.

It's also good to look for trade groups and clubs where your clients would be. If you sell business to business, these can be very diverse. For instance, if you are a worker's comp insurance company, you may want to join the builder's council because any tradesman needs to carry worker's comp for his employees and they pay quite a lot because of the danger of injury associated with the building trade. It is a great place to get leads.

Exercise 26

Join your local Chamber of Commerce or the online Chamber of Commerce if you have an Internet business.

Find networking groups in your area that you feel might be helpful for you. List a few here.

Do some research on these groups so you will know something about them before you go. If you can find a member list, you might know someone in the group who can tell you about it. Doing this will take away some of the fear associated with doing this for the first time. List the results of your initial research here.

Go to http://www.meetup.com to find new networking groups in your area. List them here.

Plan Your Appearance

Showing up at one of these events can be very stressful if you haven't had much experience at networking, unless you're prepared and have a plan. By now, you should know who your target market is and you should be able to talk about what you do specifically for your market.

Be sure to take plenty of business cards and a pen so that you can write notes on the back of business cards that are given to you.

Dress nicely but comfortably. If you can wear clothes with a pocket big enough for business cards it will be helpful as you exchange business cards. You want to appear professional at all times. Don't wear anything that might become a problem. Strong colognes can be very difficult for anyone who is allergic to perfume, so I always suggest avoiding perfumes and colognes.

Women should avoid wearing clothes that are too tight or skirts that are too short. Men need to wear well-fitting suits. These will make you self-conscious. Be sure that whatever you wear is in good repair, no missing buttons, torn hems or broken zippers. If you are distracted by what you're wearing, you won't be able to concentrate on the people you meet and they won't be able to concentrate on you.

Alert: One Super Simple Strategy

- If you could do one thing that would instantly have everyone drawn to you, would you do it?
- If it would make people smile at you, talk to you, like you, and instantly trust you, would you promise to do it regularly every time that you walk into a group of strangers?
- If it would make you feel better and happier, would you do it?
- If it could take away any negatives about the way you are dressed would you do it?

Who wouldn't?

I've seen this one thing change the destiny of many people, in both their personal lives and their business lives. If you were to stand four strangers in front of someone and you were the only one to do this, they would choose you every time. It has a 100% success rate.

What is this miracle strategy? It's so simple that you will hate me and instantly be angry, but it has been proven statistically to work. SMILE! Sometimes the simplest things work and we just need to get back to basics!

By the way, a side effect of smiling is that it is impossible to be in a bad mood when you smile. There is scientific evidence that smiling actually increases the body's production of endorphins. So it isn't just psychological, it is physical.

Now that you are smiling, let's get back to the subject. It is important to remember that although you want to build your business, you aren't there to hit-and-run. By that I mean that it isn't all about you. It's about meeting new people, learning about them, and trying to find ways to help them.

Additional Tips for Networking Events

Once again, remember your business cards! Never go to an event without a stack of business cards. Find out if you can display brochures and information about your business. Sometimes you can "rent" a small space for an extra charge. In some cases you can sponsor some part of the event which gives you the right to do a 60 second commercial (presentation) for your business.

Be sure to smile and appear friendly. Don't look as though you just robbed a bank and are afraid you're going to get caught. These people are not your enemies. They are part of your community and WANT to work with you so that you can both make a lot of money.

Know the movers and shakers. These are the people who seem to know everyone and have a great understanding of the importance of networking. They naturally connect people because they understand that doing this helps make people love and respect them.

Know who your specific power players are. These would be people who are in industries related to yours which you would naturally do business with. For example, if you're a wedding planner, these would be caterers, florists, printers, etc. These are people you would naturally refer people to and who would refer to you. If you can use this as a starting point when you get there, it will be much easier. Just don't hang on to them for dear life. They should be your lifeline, not your anchor. You're there to meet new people and expand your business, not to socialize.

Talk to as many new people as you can. If you already know everyone in your related industries, stretch! You never know where a referral will come from. You may meet someone who you have a synergy with who just wants to help you, or who knows people who can use your help.

Attend several networking events per week to keep your name and company name in view. As you will learn in the later chapters in this book, it takes more than one introduction before your name will be remembered in many cases. What I find interesting is that as you attend more of these events, you will start to run into some of the same people. This is great! If you can align yourself with them, they will connect you with other events that may be good for you. It also becomes much easier when you know more people.

Plan to meet six new people at each event. This is easy to accomplish. Take a deep breath, catch someone's eye, and introduce yourself with a smile. Be interested in who they are. If you don't understand what they do, ask them. You know how to find a company's identity, so ask them the same questions that you asked yourself earlier in this book to identify your own business. As you start to understand what they do, begin to think about anyone that you know who might be able to use their services. Let them know that you are interested in helping them. There is a caveat here. You may not feel comfortable with everyone that you meet. If you don't, that's okay. Do your best to be interested in them, then move on to the next person.

You should also look for common interests that you share with the people in your networking group. It may be something as simple as the fact that your kids go to the same school or that you both love to bowl, or that you both are extremely detail oriented or germ phobic. Whatever it is, the more people you can build bonds with, the better your business will get. Be sure to be genuine!

Know how to begin and end a conversation. Letting them know that you are interested in who they are and what they do will carry you a long way. After you've spoken, particularly when you feel you've talked about as much as you can without uncomfortable pauses, it's time to end the conversation. The best way to do this is to say "Thanks for taking the time to tell me about yourself and your business. I have a couple of other people that I need to meet." If it is someone who you want to spend additional time with, you might say "It would be great if we can get together this week so I can learn more about your business". Then agree to contact them and do so after the event is over.

Get involved in high visibility committees. The best way to be recognized is to be considered a team player who wants to help improve the entire organization. Involvement shows commitment, and come on and admit it - don't we all want to see other people committed to something that could help us even if we aren't?

Be involved in community service groups. There are many community service groups. Some of them are national and some have been started in the community to provide for a specific need that someone realized was critical. Rotary, Kiwanis, United Way, Lion's Club, YMCA and the Red Cross are just a few of the national groups. There are also church groups and a host of local charities to choose from. Call your local Chamber of Commerce or google it online to find some that may be of interest to you.

Try to be the first one at a networking event and the last one to leave. Getting there early allows you time to be sure and speak with those you really want to meet. Leaving late means that if you missed someone, you might still catch them. You may even have time for a longer conversation over a cup of coffee.

Finally, follow up with the people that you meet within 24 hours. There are some great ways to do this. I will talk more about this in a minute.

Schedule one on ones with each of the people that you meet. Never make the assumption that someone can't help you just because of the industry that they are in. Some people are natural referrers and seem to have an endless stream of contacts. Spending time with them to find out more about their business can be extremely beneficial to you. BNI has a belief that Givers Gain and that is extremely true! Nothing bonds someone to you more than if you help them. It builds trust instantly because they know that you don't have to help them. If you find ways to help them without expecting anything in return, your business will explode.

Another great follow up tip is to carry around attractive postcards with postage attached. After you meet someone, go to your car and immediately fill out the postcard with a personal note or a request to meet for coffee or lunch and put it in the mailbox. Phone calls work, but they tend to be hit or miss. These days it's really difficult to get someone on the phone, and when you do they may be distracted with whatever they are doing at the time.

I'm assuming that you have a good contact tracking system by now. Protect your contact list with your life. Some day that list may be worth selling to a new owner for your company. It is important to frequently contact your list of contacts.

Exercise 27

Start to systematically work through this section, reading and repeating the tips for successful networking until you feel you know what to do.

Schedule and plan your first networking event. List it here.

Be sure to meet at least 6 people at the event. List them here.

Track the results of your different B&B statements, and sort and log in the information about your new contacts.

Follow up with the people you meet, and schedule one on ones with the people you have just met. If it's possible, try to meet with two each day to talk more about your business and to find out more about theirs. This can be difficult if you are working in your business, but there is always lunchtime. Why not eat and talk at the same time? List at least 5 one to ones that you schedule.

Referrals

Referrals are the Super Miracle Grow of business. The easiest client to get is one that comes from a referral. Even if you've spent your life living in a cave, you are probably familiar with the concept of referrals. A referral is a way of telling someone else about someone or something that you were really happy with, and that you would recommend to the other person. It is generally the enthusiasm in the referrers voice that seals the deal and makes them contact you.

I'm sure that the cavemen originated the idea of referrals. I can imagine how that happened. Ugh says she wants better wood for her fire, and Uhn tells her that the woodsman two caves to the west has some that burns much longer and costs less. She says it all with enthusiasm in her grunts and her counterpart can't resist. It probably would have started out of necessity, but it is just as cherished today as it would have been back in those days.

From a business stand point there is nothing sweeter in the world than a referral. It cuts your building- trust- and- credibility time to almost nothing. The person who refers you wouldn't refer you if they didn't trust you, and that is generally conveyed to the person they tell about you. It's the equivalent of putting a halo over your head.

We all hope for referrals. As a matter of fact, when we are in business, we crave them! It helps us build our businesses, and it also validates us as being good at what we do. It is further proof that we are experts at what we do. It's like a long distance hug from those who love us for our knowledge. It doesn't get much better than that!

This is a good time to think back to times when you've been given referrals. Wasn't it just wonderful? It probably made you feel loved and valued, and there is no bigger compliment to receive. It's a way of not only telling other people that you did a great job, but also of saying that they have complete confidence that you will do the same for everyone.

Who Can You Call Right Now?

It's a great idea to take some time and think about all of your family and friends and contacts from other areas of your life. Then look at your past and current clients. Think about who has given you referrals and who hasn't. Make some notes and schedule some time to investigate.

Some of us don't understand why we don't get more referrals. We worry that maybe we aren't good enough. We are almost afraid to ask because we are afraid that they will tell us that they didn't like us as much as we thought they did.

The truth is, it probably doesn't have anything to do with whether we are good or not. The truth is, many people either don't think about giving referrals or are afraid to give referrals.

Let's look at both of those a little more closely. You do a great job for a client. He tells you that he is very grateful for what you've done for him. You leave and think he is going to tell everyone that he knows about you. You sit back and wait to hear from someone he knows, begging for your business. It never happens. You can't figure out why.

In the first situation, you have the Isolated Business Owner.

Here's what he is doing. He is relieved because you solved a problem for him. He is always stressed and now only has 17 more problems to deal with. Most of these problems he'll need to solve on his own. He goes back into his solitude and never thinks about you again until he either has another problem that you can solve or until he runs into you somewhere. In truth, he doesn't see very many people other than his clients, and when he is with his clients he is focused on performing his service, not on helping anyone else. He has never heard of a networking group, or if he has, he doesn't like them.

The second situation involves the Fearful Business Owner.

He is very happy with your work and finds it a pleasant surprise. He goes away saying that if he has another problem he'll give you another "try". That word should speak volumes to you. He has been burned so many times that he thinks it is a fluke that you did a good job. He can't tell anyone about you yet, because he isn't sure that you can repeat that performance. Time goes on. He uses your services several more times, and he is always happy with your company. You know he always calls you when he needs someone, so you expect he'll refer other people to you. He doesn't. He's not telling you that he's afraid to refer anyone to anyone, because if you don't live up to what he says, then he looks bad and he gets grief from the person he referred you to. He thinks that you work well for him because you and he have a sort of friendship and you give him better service than you give other people.

Can They Be Fixed?

So what's the answer? Can we change the habits of these clients?

The answer is "yes!"

There are two ways to change this. Remember the old V-8 commercials? I should have had a V-8? This is a modified version of that. Many times this person will say: "I should have given you a referral".

It's a kind of one-two punch meant to lovingly slap them in the head, and change both your business AND theirs.

The first punch is done like this:

We all have heard that the best way to get a referral is to give a referral. That means that you should always have your eye out for someone that you can introduce to someone else. Look for someone to refer to this client of yours. This is not enough, because giving a referral is only part of the solution.

If you refer someone to your client in their business, they might rethink their own nonexistent policy on referrals, but it probably won't be quite enough to move them over the edge. Here's why:

For the Isolated Business Owner, this is new territory. It makes him think about coming out of his isolation, although he may or may not actually do it. He might even plan some referrals, but never actually talks to that person about you, because he doesn't talk to anyone about his business.

For the Fearful Business Owner, he appreciates the referral, and notes that you are different than he is. He probably tells you that he appreciates the referral and won't let you down. He's too embarrassed to tell you that he still won't refer you or why because he doesn't want you to know how cynical he really is.

You can identify each one by what they say or don't say.

The Isolated Owner doesn't speak. He appreciates the business, but referrals are such a foreign concept to him that he doesn't appreciate the gift that you have given to him. He doesn't realize that you are trusting him.

The Fearful Owner expresses things in a slightly negative tone. He thinks that although you have given him a referral, it was just a fluky thing and it won't happen again. He won't feel the need to call and thank you. If he sees you he might remember to say thanks.

Since you know why they do what they do, you can help them to change what they do. Referring someone to them was the punch that got their attention.

Now it's time for the second shot to reinforce the importance of referrals.

Call them after you give them the referral. The beginning of the conversation can be done in a couple of different ways. You can ask them how it went with the referral that you gave them. Did they do work for them, how was it, did he like the client? If you have talked to the person that he did the work for and they were happy with him, you can tell him that you appreciate him taking such good care of this person because they are important to you. You can reinforce it by saying that you never give referrals unless you are sure that the person you refer will do a great job and you were sure that the client would be happy with them.

Then continue the conversation by talking to them about the importance of referrals to your business. Explain to them how referrals help you to take better care of all of your clients, because you can spend less time marketing and more time doing what you love. Explain that you can also spend less money on advertising, which helps keep your costs down, allowing you to either charge less or to give your clients more.

This next part should be a gentle conversation. You can ask them if they were unhappy with your work. When they tell you that you are wonderful, quietly mention that you were concerned about that because most of your clients give you referrals, so you wanted to check with him to be sure that he was happy with your work.

You can tell him that you give referrals whenever you find a professional who is good and that you do this for two reasons.

First, you do it because you've found that it makes you happy whenever you have received a referral, and that you usually have instant trust and credibility with this person you are referred to because they know someone who knows you.

Second, you do it because when someone asks you for someone who can do something specific, and you are able to refer someone to this person that you care about, you also help the person who needed that professional, because you solved a problem for them. Tell him that you hope that he will refer people that he knows to you, and promise to take care of them so that he is never embarrassed.

Follow up by continuing to send him referrals whenever you can, calling him as soon as you give the referral, telling him a little bit about the client so that he knows what to expect. This is a Givers Gain strategy. You may never get a referral from him. If you don't, don't worry about it. You'll get them from somewhere else. There is only one time when I would suggest that you stop giving him referrals. That time would come if you were to meet someone else who does exactly what he does and who actually does give you referrals. Ultimately, it is only logical that we must take care of those who take care of us.

Finding Referrals

Referrals come in all shapes and sizes. I've referred people around the world in realms that I thought would never need each other. Here are some of the places you can look for referrals:

Current clients – Let your clients know that you always appreciate referrals and tell them that if they can cut down on your marketing time, you'll have more time for them! Explain that marketing can be very expensive, and referrals help you to save money so that you can keep your prices where they are.

Future clients – Those that you know who are currently not ready for your services, but may know others who are. These are more difficult to get, because they may not trust you yet. Even if they do, without firsthand experience, they may not know exactly how you work.

Family and Friends – I've found that for the most part these are not always great referral sources. Sometimes it's because your family and friends don't understand exactly what you do. In some cases, it's because they make promises about what you will do and how much you will do it for. You need to approach these with caution to be sure that both of you understand each other.

Sales Professionals – Successful sales people are trained to think about referrals. It's second nature to them. Form relationships with a few good sales people and you'll build your client base more quickly. If you can't find a networking group that is bringing you the referrals that you want, then form your own group. Certainly sales professionals have a good understanding of the value of referrals.

Former co-workers – These people know your abilities. If you contact them and let them know about your area of expertise, they will refer clients to you when they find someone who has need of your specialty. They will require a little more follow up than some referral sources because they are busy in their own realm, which probably doesn't require thinking about marketing if they are still working for an employer.

Competitors – People who are in your same industry who have another area of expertise are wonderful prospects for referrals to you – not only that, but you'll have someone to refer those clients that aren't right for you. They know what they can or cannot do. They know when they might be in over their heads. Make a deal with them and tell them that you will be happy to send them clients who are in their area of expertise. This can be a really great relationship!

Related Industries – People who you might deal with who do not compete with you but who you may sometimes work alongside. For instance, if you are a real estate agent, you will deal with mortgage brokers, home inspectors, appraisers, title companies, etc. They are all good sources of referrals. It is important to really impress them with your abilities before they will put themselves out for you.

Train yourself to listen for opportunities to refer someone else. You need to sharpen your listening skills and always be ready to help. The more that you give, the more that you will get. Make it a point to really get to know other business owners. When you have any work done, take notice of how the company performs. You will be much more careful about who you will hire, and you will be able to tell people a lot more about them when you do recommend them.

There is one more thing to know about referrals. When you refer someone to someone else, if it's possible, arrange to introduce them to each other. If you can't do that, be sure to call the person that you have referred someone to, and tell that person about the person and the issue that requires help. It's also helpful if you explain to the company how you described them to the client so that they know what you think about them.

In most cases, it is better to ask the client if you can give their phone number to the company that you are referring to them. Then you can call the company directly, let them know that this is a referral from you, and give the company as much background about the client and their situation as possible.

Follow up first with the client and then with the company to be sure that everyone is happy. You'll want to do this within a few days to a week, depending on the urgency of the client's need.

Exercise 28

Think of 5 people that you can refer to other people List them here.

Think of 5 people who you can ask for referrals, either current or past clients, family and friends, or past business contacts. List them here.

Schedule a time to meet or call them. If they aren't familiar with your business, explain to them what you do. Ask them for referrals. Write the results here.

Testimonials

Since testimonials are continuous referrals, we need to talk about the benefits of these now.

A testimonial is a written or taped referral that you can use with the permission of the person who gave it to you. This easier than asking for a referral and almost as wonderful. In some cases it's better because if you use them appropriately, you get even more business than you will with a referral. It's easier because they don't need to brainstorm who they know.

Sometimes people have reasons for not talking about your services to other people, so they don't give you any referrals. It may be that they are busy enough that they don't focus on business building, or they may be an Isolated Business Owner. Since you are focused on business building, and you don't want to wait and hope for a referral, ask them for a testimonial.

Testimonials can be done using different types of information, but the end effect is that as a result of what these people say, other people will want to use your service. They can talk about how much they like your company, the benefit they received from your service, the problem you solved for them, or the fact that you are honest and ethical. They are always presented in superlatives, whether spoken or implied.

IMPORTANT! **You must update your posted testimonials from time to time, particularly if they are posted on the internet.** The Federal Trade Commission is rabid about checking testimonials online to be sure that they are recent.

When you complete a job for a client, you will obviously check in with him to ascertain that he was happy. You can do this with a phone call. You can do it with a survey. You can do it in person. The important thing is that when you check in with them, and they tell you they are happy, you must ask them for a testimonial.

If they filled out a survey form and you liked what they said, ask them if you can use it as a testimonial and put it on your website or in your printed material or wherever you decide to use it.

If it is verbal, ask them if you can put it in writing and send it to them to be sure it's correct and then use it. They may want to write it themselves, and that's great. The key is to make sure that they do it.

Sometimes people will even be willing to do an audio or video testimonial. From my personal experience, they tend to be more willing to do audio. It is less work and they don't need to worry about their appearance, etc. In addition, audio has the advantage of voice inflections and excitement without the visual which might be distracting if they have spinach in their teeth (smile).

Many people are well-meaning and are willing to give you a testimonial, but the truth is that they will never get around to doing it. If that is the case, there is a way to get this done. When you check in with a client after the work has been completed, and they tell you that they are happy with your work, if they are enthusiastic, make notes of what they say, using their words. Ask if they would be willing to give you a testimonial. If they say yes, thank them and tell them that you will be anxiously awaiting it. Give it a few days.

If you don't get it within a few days, either they have forgotten or they just don't have time. Write it out for them and send it as an attachment. Tell them that you value their time, and that this is what you remember them saying to you about the work that was done. Ask if you can use it the way it is, or invite them to change anything that they'd like to change. Follow this up with a brief phone call the next day to get a final answer.

Testimonials will get you a great deal of business, so don't be afraid to ask for one! Nothing is more effective than having someone else toot your horn for you. Ask if you can put it up on your website with their company name.

Exercise 29

Who can you ask for a testimonial? List them here, then schedule the call and do it!

If you have no one to ask for testimonials, offer to give away your services to 5 people provided they give you a testimonial when they are satisfied with your service. List them here.

Upload the testimonials to your website immediately!

Education/Information

This is an important touch to include in your marketing approach and much of your marketing should be based around educating your market. We discuss it in different forms throughout the book. What makes people understand that you are an expert is this form of touch. After networking it is the second most important.

Educating and informing all of your prospects will tell them everything that they need to know to decide whether you are enough of an expert to provide a service to them, and whether you are offering the right service for them.

Let's talk about the difference between education and information.

Education

Education means that you give them your knowledge. Teach everyone what you know. Many experts are afraid to do this, because they are afraid that they won't be needed if they do this. One of my mentors, Eben Pagan, taught me to give away the best that I have for FREE. He is right. You can give away your best and clients will run to you. It is such a "wow" moment for them that they want to work with you because you gave them something wonderful. It demonstrates that you are confident in your own abilities and that you aren't afraid that you will lose clients.

Sometimes by educating the public, you make them understand that they really do need your service! Imagine that. You just created a client. I've seen this happen many times. It may be that a generator isn't even on a consumer's radar, but if an electrician explains the benefits of having a generator, and mentions a problem this solves that the consumer can identify with, the consumer realizes that the electrician has the solution to a problem. You see, the consumer always thought about generators for hurricanes, and he didn't worry about hurricanes. He does have a problem with his electric going out during the summer when usage is high and his electric provider shuts down different areas to conserve energy. Now the consumer has a generator and the electrician has a new client who will always call him for any electrical need because he solved a problem for him.

I've also learned that when you give away what you think is your best, you really have more to offer to your clients than you think. They will get more out of what you teach them after they become clients, because you really ARE an expert, and you have incredible value. I am amazed every day at the things that other business owners teach me about what they do. I am equally amazed at what my clients teach me! That's why I refuse to stop doing individual and group coaching. I get to learn for free!

You can provide education for prospects either verbally or in writing, individually or in groups. Although it is easier to do in writing, because you can distribute it at will, speaking is more powerful, because the audience gets a better feel for who you are. How you do it is completely up to you, and I suggest that you do it in as many ways as you possibly can.

Some of the best methods:
Speeches
Ebooks
Articles
Blogs
Videos

Information

Your prospects also need to know what you can do for them, how you will do it, and why you do it.
This is the reason that you should provide brochures, videos, and any other means of getting across what your company is all about.

How can someone buy your product or service if they don't understand it? If you provide them with a description of your services, they will instantly be able to recognize when you are the one that they need.

You can do videos showing what you do. You can feature your office, your equipment, your vehicles, your employees, and anything else that demonstrates your business identity.

This is also a great place to tell your core story – why you do what you do. Powerful stories will get you a remarkable amount of business. You must be sincere.

Information can be given in many forms. Below are the most popular:
    Brochures
    Website
    Videos

Writing

This one is more complicated because there is so much to it. Writing includes everything, from web copy to article writing to your company brochure. Very few business owners are really good at writing their own copy, yet they are very seldom happy with copy they pay for.

I believe that you have to find the right help for the right job. That really means that you want one person to do your brochure copy and another to form your website in the proper manner.

Article Writing

It is wonderful if you can write some articles of your own. They need to be a minimum of 350 words, which is not very much. If you can't write your own, you can hire a ghostwriter to write articles for you on any subject you choose. It's quite inexpensive and if done correctly, will truly position you as an expert in your industry.

There are a few things that you need to think about before you sit down to write your article.
   • Your Subject
   • Interesting Title
   • Body of the Article
   • Who Will Publish It

It is always easiest to write about the things that you know. If you can back it up with some provable facts or statistics then it has more validity because it is not just your opinion. That is not to say that an opinion/ editorial piece has no value. It can, particularly if you are writing about a subject that it really getting a lot of press right now and happens to fall into your category. You will want to approach it from an angle that is interesting and that hasn't been written about before. It shouldn't be too far out, unless that is your target market.

The title is extremely important. If your title doesn't grab the attention of the reader, it will never be read. Find a few words that sum up what the article is about. Use big action words and superlative adjectives to create interest. Be sure that the reader knows what he will learn when he reads it. You are once again appealing to your bullseye market, those who are interested in what you have to offer. You can
- peak their curiosity by putting it in the form of a question,
- make a statement then supply the evidence,
- make a promise to teach something then educate them

Before you write the article, you want to think about who will publish it for you. If you are going to submit it to a specialty site, you will want to write the article to appeal specifically to that group of people.

You can write and post to the web on many sites. The most popular is http://www.ezinearticles.com . A distant second is http://ideamarketers. com . Both are free, and although they have some restrictions, they will certainly post most articles. When you post there, you include a short biography describing who you are and how you can be contacted. If you know of someone online who compliments you and has a newsletter, you can ask them if they would use your articles on their sites and in their newsletters as long as they post your byline with it, which just gets your name out to more people. It also helps your website rank to have articles on your website, so you definitely want to have some unique articles on your site that you haven't given to anyone else.

Submit your articles to any online of the numerous online directories that you can find. Sometimes it is helpful if you change the article just a little bit before you submit it to multiple directories. It may get used more often this way.

Local Market Offline

If you are a local professional, and want to reach just your local market, contact your newspaper and local trade magazines. Getting an article printed there will give you instant expert status. The alternative is to ask them to do an article about you or an aspect of what you do. Some newspapers are always looking for something interesting to write about, and if you fit that description, you can find your face in print.

You might also try to submit an article to a local advertising paper. If you can convince the owner that it will give his readers something else to look at, you might get some free space. You may have to buy some ad space to get this opportunity. If it is inexpensive, it might be worth trying depending on the number of readers it has. If you can do a regular column in any of these, you will become memorable, even to those who don't read it as they see your name week after week. In a perfect world, you will have some people who look forward to reading your column. This kind of exposure can make you a local household name, and can really push your career forward.

Blogging

Another writing strategy is to add a blog to your site or to start a separate site for your blog so that interested potential and current clients can read what you have to say. They get to know you better this way, and your perfect clients will start showing up. Write about something around your specialty area. This helps you to position yourself as the expert and builds your credibility. You need to be dedicated to regularly posting to your blog to keep the interest of your followers. As always, it is best if you can give them something that they didn't know before and find interesting.

You can publish tips about any subject. Once you assemble that list, you can distribute it to your current clients and potential clients. You can distribute it at events and networking groups and anywhere that you do presentations.

If you decide to start a separate site for your blog, you can do this by going to either wordpress.com or typepad.com. Both of these have a free version and plenty of templates to choose from. Wordpress has become the more popular site. Look at both of them to decide what features are important to you. You will also need a separate domain name. The easiest domain to choose and to get is to use whatever your domain name is, followed by "blog". In other words, had I done that for successfanatic.com, it would have been successfanaticblog.com. You can then connect it to your site by placing the link on your site, or by having a "blind link" that doesn't appear on the site, but it takes you there directly. In return, if you put a link on your blog to your main site, you won't lose a reader who wanders away from your main site and goes to your blog. This link can also be a blind link.

How good are your blogging skills?

There are entrepreneurs who have started blogging and have become so successful at it, that in the end, they don't need to do anything else! They do this by building their readership to big numbers then finding sponsors for their sites. The best sponsors are those who are not directly recommended by the blog owner, but who can advertise their product on the site and make substantial amounts of money in the process.

There is one reminder I have for professionals when it comes to writing. Many times business owners would rather write than meet people. It is a very comforting feeling to just talk to an imaginary audience rather than facing real people. It is a nice fantasy world where you can believe that everyone loves listening to your advice. However, there is no more powerful and faster way to build rapport than by getting out and actually meeting new people and talking to others whom you know. Writing as your only strategy can't be used to find new customers. It requires a mix of all of these strategies.

Regular Ezine

These days most people expect that you will contact them by email. In the old days, businesses used to send out newsletters by mail. Now, you can do it in one click on the internet. Every business should be sending out a newsletter at least once a month. This will help you to stay fresh in the minds of your clients and potential clients, and to tell them what you have to offer them right now. You should always have something going on that they can either take advantage of, or tell their contacts about. This is a great business building technique.

Your ezine should have one main article, followed by your calendar of events and one short tip. It doesn't need to be overly long, and it's better if it isn't. If it is too long, it won't be read.

Be sure that your information is relevant to them and that it is current. It is a great time to once again prove your status as an expert.

Exercise 30

Start a blog and have it added to your site or start a separate site at http://www.wordpress.com or http://www.typepad.com . If you do a separate blog, list the name of the domain here.

List the subject of your blog and the subject of your first three blogs.

Write an article and have it published either online or in a local or trade publication that is appropriate for your service. The article should be between 350 and 700 words long.
List the title and where you'll publish it.

Hire someone to write for you if you can't do either of the above. List appropriate candidate names here.

Brainstorm a name for your company ezine. List appropriate topics to write about for the next 3 months.

Information

Writing your list of services

Because it is part of your marketing plan, I felt that this was a good place to talk about writing the list of services that you will make available to your clients. You always want to list your best things singularly at a price that is a little high. You want them to be listed at least at the minimum amount you want to earn from a client. Then put together packages of services that demonstrate a better bargain for the client, although they will be more than the singular items.

Do this so that you can encourage the higher dollar tickets, making it cost less to buy a package of three than two single items. If you are an air conditioning company the client might pay $75 for a visit and $90 to have their ducts cleaned. If they buy your annual package, they will get both of those and a free air filter change for $160 total.

When you are concentrating on prices, please remember that if they can't afford you, they shouldn't be a customer. As we've discussed before, don't underprice your services because you are afraid that you won't have enough business. If you are good at what you do, then you deserve to be paid. If you can build the ticket higher by offering them a good value, then it is a win-win for both of you.

Another alternative is to give them a base package, then have add-on items to build the ticket. For example, if you are an air conditioning professional, you can do basic annual and a daytime emergency service (two times per year) for $125. Then you can do an add on four air filter changes per year for an additional $40, and/or an emergency repair package for an additional $65 which would cover no parts, only labor and would be limited to 2 emergency visits. They must take the basic package to get either of the other two. In other words, they couldn't get the 2 free emergency visits unless they bought the package. For many people, this alone would be worth the $190 it would cost when you buy the basic package for $125 then add the emergency package for $65.

Lastly, list different packages, making the most expensive one the best value. In other words, in the same air conditioning company example, the basic package which is 2 regular visits would be $125, the premium package would be 2 regular visits and 4 filter change visits for $160, and the platinum package would be the premium package (2 regular visits and 4 filter changes) plus 2 emergency visits (labor only) for $225. This is clearly a great deal for the client, especially one who has an older system and knows that it is just a matter of time until they have an unexpected breakdown. As a condition of purchasing your top dollar package, you may want to limit the service to clients who have systems that are less than a certain age so that you don't have clients who limp their systems along longer than they should.

It is important to have your sales or service people thoroughly and carefully explain the scope of what your service will cover so that there are no disappointments later on. If it is in writing and you've given it to them, explained it to them, and they signed it, there will be no disputes as long as you've written it properly. You might want them to sign an acknowledgement that it was explained to them.

Show it to several clients or to anyone who may not know exactly what you do. Ask them if they understand what it means. If you start to do business, and someone points out that something is not clear, be prepared to rethink the language and find a way to fix it immediately. If one person doesn't understand it, there will also be others who don't understand it. Since it will be a legal agreement, you will also want to have your attorney put his stamp of approval on it. That way he will be prepared to defend it if there is ever a problem.

Brochures

Now that you have your core story and your list of services, you should be able to put together a good brochure to be used appropriately.

I don't believe in being overly dependent on printed materials, because nothing can build trust except you. However, sometimes a properly written brochure can be another tool to help you convince potential clients to use your service.

There are different schools of thought on formats for effective copy. I believe that the brochure should describe the problem that you'll solve and the benefit of using your service over any other service. It's great if it is personalized and shows you and your staff. Most important are testimonials from happy clients. A testimonial is the fastest way to build trust and credibility because it's someone else telling the reader that you're terrific. Using their photo is very effective.

Color brochures are more often read more than black and white. The brochures should be standard size on good quality paper.

If you are selling Business To Business then you might want to consider a professionally designed brochure. Hire a graphic designer and copywriter and set a budget in advance.

To decide the appropriate content for your brochure, look at other brochures and choose what you want included in your brochure. You may want an attention getting caption with your logo on the front, a great description of your business services on the inside with testimonials and your bio on the back. That's just one suggestion. You (and your designer if you use one) will have to determine what's best for you and for your company when you get to that point.

There is another consideration when using a graphic designer. Get a price before awarding them the job. Prices for graphic design work varies wildly, depending on experience, ability, financial need and the ego of the artist. Be sure that they schedule at least three meetings with you so you can be sure that you are both on the same page.

You will be asked to provide copy before they start, which you need to get to them so that they can do their work. The pictures and design will be based on what you want to say. This will take up some of your time, so you want to think about it before you even hire the designer. If you aren't capable of writing copy, you will need to hire someone to write it with your help. You will need to give them a good idea of what you want to convey to your customer so they can best represent your company. This is easy if you are able to concentrate on a specific aspect of your business. If it is a general brochure, it can be more difficult. Your designer can probably suggest some copywriters who can help you.

Exercise 31

Consider your business and think about when you might use a brochure. Do you need a brochure?

What will you tell potential clients in your brochure?

Where will you use these brochures?

Is a brochure necessary or would a flier be more useful?

Write down the basic ideas you want communicated in your brochure.

If necessary, find a graphic artist to design your brochure. Be as detailed as possible when talking to him to be sure he understands the project. List your candidates below.

Spend time writing your exact list of services. Think of every service you will perform and put a price to it.

Develop a list of "packaged services" that will allow your clients to benefit from these combinations by getting better value. List your packages here.

Demonstration

Promotional Events

Promotional events are a superb way to display your business in a very professional setting, particularly if you use some imagination when you do it.

For example, if you are a contractor of any type, the local home show is a great place to showcase your business. I've been to enough of them to know that you can find some great products and services there. However, the guy who gives me some useful knowledge will be on top of my list unless someone is there who does something totally outrageous to get my attention.

There are some great examples of wonderful promotions done at events. For example, the guys who staged a skit about rushing and being stressed and quite literally yelled and screamed as they came in the hall, then walked over to the hot tub they had set up and got in, where he completely relaxed and appeared to be in his own private Nirvana, really painted a visual picture that I still haven't forgotten to this day. Not only that, but I told everyone about what a cool and imaginative company they are. They made me believe, in that two minute show, that they think differently and aren't afraid to do whatever it takes to get my business.

Private Events

It is easy to have someone hire you to do a 10 to 30 minute presentation. Most service groups are always looking for speakers who will teach them something that they don't know. This is your time to shine and to proof to your audience that you are truly an expert. Remember the research that you did for your direct mail pieces? Once again you can use them here, to teach this audience and to make them say "wow" at least five times. If you do that, you will always instantly pick up business.

Statistics show that at any time, no more than 3% a normal audience will require what you have to offer. However, there is 7% of an audience who is thinking about what you offer, and if you give them a "wow" presentation, then they will not even consider anyone else when they are ready. There is another 30% who may need you in the future, who will become part of your target market and will also remember you.

Speakers who hold seminars sometimes like to bring in guest speakers who know about areas they don't. Although they generally are reluctant to pay you to speak at their seminar, it is great exposure to new prospects in a setting where the participants have already shown that they are willing to spend money for what they need. Just be sure that if you are a guest speaker that you will add true value to your audience and you aren't there just to pitch their product or service.

Mini-Presentations

Booking a room to hold a mini presentation can be a great way to introduce prospective clients to your services. Find a subject that is getting a lot of attention and give your ideas on how to solve the problem. If this is a subject that you know inside out, and that you have thoroughly researched, you will be able to answer questions from the group. Once again, back up what you have to say with statistics and facts that your audience will find valuable.

These presentations can also be done by telephone (teleseminars) or computer (webinars). Any of the forms of a presentation have their pros and cons, which you will soon discover. Everyone wants to get an education, and they will commit to being present but they will not show up. Life is very busy for everyone, and it is difficult for those who work to fit everything into their schedules. When you are calculating your attendance, it is safe to calculate a 50% show rate, even when you charge for the presentation. This is nothing against you or your abilities. It is just the way life is for many people. We all think that we can do more than we can.

How To Pack Your Mini-Presentation with Anxious Buyers

So where will you find people who are interested in what you have to say? This is not as difficult as you think, provided that you remember the statistics that I've given you in this book. Frist, only 3% will be in the market at any given time. Second, another 6 to 7% is thinking about it. Third, only about 50% will show up to learn about it even after they tell you they will be there.

Now you know that you really need to invite a lot of people to fill your room. Let's start with the obvious avenues for your invitations.

Your contact list
A targeted mailing list
A targeted email list
Local advertising (local seminar)
Your power group (local seminar)
Joint ventures (teleseminars/webinars)
Affiliates (teleseminars/webinars)

This list is only limited by the number of people that you think of who would be willing to promote you.

Another outlet would be through a nonprofit who fits with your subject matter. If you donate some of the proceeds, most charitable organizations are willing to help you.

Exercise 32

Find events either in your community or in your industry that will allow you to promote your service. In some areas you can use your local library meeting rooms for free. List some possibilities here.

Schedule one event per quarter if possible. Organize and list the things you'll need to accomplish for this event.

Brainstorm names of peopke and organizations who can help you to promote your seminar.

Public Speaking Tips

We've already talked about this in the last chapter. It is a great way for an accountant, attorney, coach, chiropractor, etc. to become known. These opportunities include:

Chamber of Commerce meetings
BNI or other networking groups
Trade conventions
Service organizations
Community colleges and trade schools
Local clubs
Radio interviews
TV interviews

You can start your own local radio or television show. Radio is easier since you don't need to film it ahead of time. Now you can also do Blog Talk Radio on the Internet (www.blogtalkradio.com).

If you don't have a lot of experience speaking in public, you may want to join Toastmasters to get some experience. There are local chapters everywhere which meet every week just for the purpose of practicing their speaking techniques. They are a very supportive group and help you to improve without criticism.

10 Ways To Keep Your Audience Interested

1. Know your material. This builds your credibility as an expert. Be sure to have all of your facts on the tip of your tongue as though you do this every day.
2. Smile. When you look confident and demonstrate that you love your subject, the audience will want to work with you.
3. Look some of the audience members directly in the eye. If you focus on a few different people, you show friendliness. Try to catch the eye of those who appear disinterested in order to pull them in.
4. Move. Use arm gestures and move around the stage as discussed below.
5. Show personality onstage. If something goes wrong, acknowledge it and laugh about it.
6. Use voice inflections. Monotone will put your audience to sleep faster than Brahm's lullaby.
7. Use visual aids. Most people (70%) are visual learners and they tend to remember what they see rather than what they hear.
8. Tell them stories that they can relate to. The best way to concrete a new memory is to tell a story to go along with it.
9. Give them their WOWs.
10. Be funny if you can. Humor makes it easy to remember facts, and gives them a positive memory of you.

Generally, your speech won't be more than 5 or 10 minutes. It doesn't need to be long, just informative and entertaining.

Setting a Reaction

If you are speaking on a stage, it is possible to control the mood of your audience just by changing where you stand on the stage. This is how it's done.

When you first come out onto the stage, come out with high energy and go directly to the center of the stage. Ask those questions that require a "yes" answer (Do you want to know how you can increase your income by 40% this year?) Make sure they give you enthusiastic answers.

Move to one side of the stage to talk about thoughtful things. Ask questions that make them think.

Walk to the other side to talk about the solution to the problem. Every time you go to one particular side you will be able to get the same reaction. One side will be the thoughtful side. They will start to think before you even get there. The other side is the solution side. They will be relieved when they see you on that side.

Therefore, when you want them to buy at the end of the talk, you'll go back to the center of the stage again, where they said yes to all of your questions in the beginning, and where you want them to say yes to buying your product or service!

You can set any emotion anywhere on the stage, even setting a different emotion if you come off the stage and stand on the floor. Try doing this in your next presentation even if you don't have a stage. You can accomplish this by leaning side to side or turning your body differently.

Exercise 33

Analyze your speaking abilities. You can do this by making an audio tape of yourself doing a 5 minute speech. This will help you to know how you sound. You'll be able to know if you sound too monotone, or if you tend to repeat the same word. List any problems here.

Then make a video of yourself doing the same speech. This will help you to see the way you appear to other people. You'll be able to fix any nervous habits that appear. What are they?

If you know that this area needs work, do something about it now. Join Toastmasters in your area. It will be good practice, and they give each other constructive, gentle criticism. Get the information about your local toastmasters and write the date of your first meeting here and on your calendar.

Schedule a 2 minute speech at your local Chamber or any networking group. Write the date here.

Schedule a 10 minute speech through BNI to talk about your business. List the highlights here.

Practice using emotion- setting in different aspects of your life. It can be done in many situations, as long as you make sure that you command the emotion properly. Write your observations here

Give Aways

Educating is a give away. There are also products that are made specifically to give to prospects, current clients, or referral sources. Both of these have great value. If you have educated your market, then it is good to cement it with a promotional product that will remind them of you.

Promotional Items

Whenever you have a speaking engagement, you need to have some sort of promotional items to offer to those who attend. Promotional items come in many shapes and sizes. It may be your brochures, or a special offer for the group that you are speaking to that you put on a flyer.

Many speakers will put their company name on pens and notepads to give to the audience to take notes on. I am not a great believer in just doing promotional items of this sort unless it is specific to your company. Why spend a dollar or more per person for a gift, when it really doesn't do anything to remind them of who you are?

There are many promotional companies on the internet who will sell you whatever you want. That is, provided that you know what you want. It is better if you can work with a company who will help you to find what is specific for your company. You want something that will further brand your business.

Educational Workshops

If you go to Home Depot on any Saturday morning, you will get a good idea of an educational workshop. There is usually someone there teaching a technique for installation of something around the house. Along those same lines, a good number of service professionals offer free educational seminars where they teach them more than they can learn in a ten minute presentation that you do in front of the general public.

This will be taught to a group of people who sign up to learn what you have to teach specifically because they are interested in the subject matter. This can be almost anything. Estate attorneys have this to educate middle age and older people about what will happen to their estate when they die. CPAs will have tax seminars to talk about tax changes. Nutritionists will have seminars provide information about proper eating and vitamins to those who are concerned about health. In some cases they may even do free blood analysis. There is no obligation to purchase anything when someone attends one of these, and the listener leaves feeling better informed.

The biggest issue for many companies is to find a location to hold the presentations, since many service providers have little or no extra space. It is sometimes possible to find another business where you can hold this at no expense to you.

Exercise 34

Think about what types of products would be effective at branding your business. List some here

What types of presentations can you do to educate your market?

Where can you hold these presentation?

Chapter 7

Other Important Miracle Grow Touch Guideline Methods

Direct Contact

Any type of direct contact requires that you develop a specific plan of action ahead of time in order to carry it out correctly and efficiently.

There are 4 basic types of direct contact methods that can and should be used to generate new business.

In Person Contact
Telephone Contact
Email Contact
Mail Contact

In person, phone, and email contact generally involve little or no money. Direct mail can be very expensive, yet more people spend money on direct mail than use any of the other forms of direct contact.

The first three do require an expenditure of time, and if not planned correctly, can be very unproductive for the amount of time that you invest. If that happens to you, it means you have not planned your direct contact campaign well and are spinning your wheels. Using direct contact means that you need to work smarter, and really put some thought into what you are going to do. This applies to all forms of direct contact marketing including mail.

Personal Contact

If you are new in business, it is worth your while to do some direct contact work in person. It's a great way to reach people that you may never find in any other way.

One form of personal contact is known as "cold calling" and is generally the most hated form of marketing. This is contacting someone you've never met to see if you can convince them to buy your service. Door to door selling falls into this category. If you are a business doing business with business owners it is a little easier, because you can drop in to their business and there is a chance that they might want what you have to offer. I must admit that it was never my favorite form, but I can tell you that it is extremely effective and if used appropriately can also be very cost effective and can get you instant business.

I once had the owner of a pest control service walk into my office. I was very busy at the time, and he was sensitive to that fact. I agreed to see him. He came into my office and said: "My name is John Smith. I own ABC Pest Control." He handed me his business card and said: "Try me once and I promise you'll never use anyone else". I just stared at him waiting for the big sales pitch.

That was all he said. Nothing else. In that one sentence he conveyed confidence about his business and himself. I asked the price of his services. He was a little higher than the company that I was using, and I told him that. He said that the difference between his company and the other company is that he is no nonsense, responds quickly, has a completely efficient office staff to back him up, and does all of the work himself. So I decided to try him. He was correct, and to this day I have never used anyone else. He doesn't do the work himself anymore, but has an excellently trained staff who have now taken over the manual part of the business. He and I are still friends, and we refer people to each other frequently.

Sometimes it's just a matter of changing the way you look at these calls. One of the best examples of this is the story told by the master who looks at the world differently than most, Tony Robbins.

He tells the story of how, early in his career he was selling door to door. Statistics showed that someone would buy his product about once every 100 times. He made $1000 every time someone bought from him. He broke it down so that he figured that each call was worth $10. So every time someone said no, he didn't mind. He figured he just made another $10 and he was happy to continue knocking on doors and being refused until he got to the next interested prospect.

Some people would rather die than make a cold call. If you are adverse to cold calling, find other ways to meet people that you really want to meet. As you have seen, there are many ways to find personal contact meetings. You might also consider asking other people that you know if they know the specific people that you are trying to meet. An introduction from a third party is a stress free way to get to the same place.

Exercise 35

Think about whom may be potential clients for you. Make a list of personal contacts to visit. You should have at least 3 per week.

Think about other businesses who complement your business or whose business you compliment. Make a list of these businesses to contact and visit one of these per week.

Direct Contact by Telephone

The phone company, back when there was just one, had a great slogan. It was:

Reach out. Reach out and touch someone.

And as you see, direct contact work comes in more forms than just knocking on doors. It can also be done by telephone. Cold calls are a little less scary by phone. Ma Bell helped all of us with marketing long before any of today's marketing books were written. They are still correct. Calling someone on the telephone is a great way to initiate new business.

There are different times when you will use the telephone to approach new clients. There are three choices here.

1. Research the people you are interested in meeting, whether to take on as a client or to build a relationship with. Think about what you want to say to them ahead of time. What can you say to them to make them willing to stay on the phone with you for more than ten seconds? If you have any contacts in common, this may be a good time to mention this to them. Explain why you wanted to introduce yourself to them. Sincerity in your voice and your choice of words will be critical to the success or failure of your call. If it sounds like you've struck a chord with them, ask them if you can meet for coffee, lunch, or whatever you think you might be able to arrange.

2. Call people that you know from other areas of your life who either might be interested in your service or who might know someone else who would be. Explain that you are building your business and use your B & B Statement. Speak to them as appropriate. If you know that they may be able to use your service, tell them that you were thinking about them and would love to arrange some time for coffee so you can talk a little more. If it is someone who definitely can't use your service, tell them you would like to have coffee with them so you can show them what you are doing in case they run into someone they know who would benefit from what you do.

3. Buy lists of people who would be interested in what you have to offer. This is the least effective method of making phone calls, and there are rules about who you can and cannot call. If someone has placed themselves on the National Do Not Call List, you do not want to call them. Go to this site to learn more: https://telemarketing. donotcall.gov/

Getting Past the Gate Keeper

In many companies, the owner has a "Gate Keeper". That's usually either a secretary or an assistant whose job it is to protect them from being interrupted. The really good ones can be tough to get through and it will take some imagination to get to the prospect

It's very rare that a high powered busy executive will actually take messages from everyone, or answer the phone themselves. Sometimes you will get lucky and call on a day when the Gate Keeper is not there and a temp is filling in. You might actually have a chance on that day.

In many cases, you'll need to do some detective work to find a time and place to talk to them when their Gate Keeper isn't around. This can be anywhere the business owner goes – from the gym to a doctor's office. Be sure to really know this person, their likes and dislikes, and prepare what you'll say to them in order to catch their attention in a short amount of time. If all else fails, try humor. It doesn't work every time, but in many cases it's extremely effective. You know that you can catch more flies with homey than with vinegar, and here it is extremely true.

Another way to do this is to send him/her something really unique with a note attached that will appeal to their sense of humor. The most famous of these stories is the man who wanted to get in to see the female executive but couldn't get through her Gate Keeper. He finally sent her a coconut with a note attached that said: "You're a tough nut to crack. Please call me." She did and he sold her his product.

Also, keep in mind that many times the gatekeeper feels unappreciated and overworked. The y have to be the bad guy to a lot of people. Their boss takes them for granted and doesn't always thank them for everything that they do for them. When you are the boss's secretary, even though there may be other secretaries that work in the company, you are removed from the others because of your status. You know confidential details of the boss and the business, and you don't want to be in a situation where you might say the wrong thing and talk about a detail that gives away something that might be a problem for your boss. Consequently, the gatekeeper will not socialize with anyone else. They are starved for appositive attention or stimuli, and welcome someone who is happy and treats them well. Approach the gatekeeper with a respectful, happy professionalism, and they may be willing to help you as much as they are able. This works in a smaller office where you don't have to go through a few layers of gatekeepers to accomplish your goal. It will take some extra effort on your part, because it means that you will have to physically show up at the office. Personal meetings are always more effective than faceless phone calls, letters, or emails.

It may be that the owner is not the person that you want to see. It may be a department head who has employees that you know you can help. You want to talk to him about hiring you, but you haven't been able to get to him directly, and you don't know if he has received the information that you've sent him several times. You can use the same tactics to get to this person. The key is to be sure that you are targeting the correct person in the organization.

Think of people you know who might work for that company. It may be that you know someone who knows either the person you are trying to get to or someone close to them. At the very least, they may be able to give you some detail about that person which would help you find a way to contact them.

When you get their attention, you first want to tell them what you can do for them. This is one area where your one sentence Bullseye and Benefit Statement can really come in handy. You've just followed them to the end of the earth. You should know that your service is perfect for them. If someone has mentioned to you that they have a particular problem that you can help them with, it will probably become easy to talk to them.

Instead of using your one line B & B Statement, you can formulate it as a question. For me that would sound like this: "You know how some service companies have too few clients and end up working with clients they hate and accepting rate cuts? I teach them how to have more and better clients at higher rates. It changes their lives forever."

Exercise 36

Think about who you could call to speak to about your business. Write a phone script so that you can attract their attention quickly and keep them from hanging up. It must be sincere to not sound generic.

Target specific potential clients to introduce your service to. If you are calling individuals, be sure they are not on the do not call list. You can get information about this list online. Make a list here of the first group of five to call.

If you run into a gatekeeper, make note of the person's name. Then you can decide how to approach the gatekeeper so that they will get to know you and like you. Make notes about whatever you can learn about that person.

Direct Contact Work On The Internet.

Direct contact work can also be done on the Internet to build partnerships or to develop relationships with people who can help you by giving you referrals. Do some research to see who is online that you admire or that you feel you have some synergy with. Email them and tell them that you believe that you have some common interests or ask them some questions. Chances are good that they will answer you and you can begin to build a relationship.

Contact work by email is really nice because the person you are contacting can answer at their leisure. It's important to put a great subject in the subject line to get their attention so they will read it and answer you. This will probably take you longer than actually writing the email, but it is critical to get it right. "Can I help you _____?" can work well, provided you are sure about what they might need.

Direct contact work on the web is really beneficial because many people who are on the web have extensive lists of customers or potential customers, and can help promote you to their list. For that reason you don't want to contact people who are your direct competition. You can become allies with someone who offers something that compliments your area of expertise. This can be beneficial to both of you and will extend your reach into the global market. For example, if you are a bridal consultant, you can contact anyone who does things for brides or weddings, such as caterers, printers, etc.

Direct Contact Mail

There is also the old fashioned method of sending direct mail pieces. It can be geographical or by interest. For a while, direct mail marketing lost favor. It was considered junk mail, and was very seldom opened by anyone.

Over the last couple of years, since the advent of electronic billing and payments, people are receiving less mail so these bulk mail pieces actually get more attention than they did for a long time. This has been shown to be very successful and cost effective under the right circumstances. The bad news is that the cost of printing and postage have gotten higher, and unless you have a high dollar service and are able to target your market very specifically, it is generally not cost effective. It must be done correctly to assure success in this market. Targeting a very specific market is the only way this can be effective. There are companies which can sell you very specific mailing lists, based on your criteria. Again, you must know your bullseye market before you can be sure that you are paying for a list that will get will get you the return that you want to have.

When you are doing direct mail, many people send the prospect to a website for information. I suggest that you have them call. It is much more effective because if they are directed to a website, many people won't ever go to the site. We all start out with good intentions when we pick up our computers, but most of the time we get lost in other things when we go to the internet, whether it is email or another site. If they have to call to get a free report, and you have whet their appetite by what you have promised to tell them, they will call. That gives you the opportunity to not only get their contact information, but also to initiate a conversation with them so that you can decide if they would be a good fit for your company. If you do this, you can hire someone just to take these phone calls. That person can work from their home and receive a commission. They need to be well trained by you to say what you want them to say. There is a specific personality type this is really good on the phone, and you want to be sure that their voice is friendly, warm and reassuring.

It is possible to get a discount on postage by using bulk mail. Bulk mail is a special rate that is paid provided you have a bulk mail license. It is based on zip code and if you really do a lot of mail outs to your target market, it can save you a great deal of money over the course of a year. The direct mail services can save you money on postage by doing your mailings for you, particularly if you don't have the time or the staff to do this for you.

If you are going to do direct mail, I'd like to suggest that you use postcards. When someone doesn't have to open it, it has a better chance of being read. Make it colorful to get their attention. In the event that you do send stuffed envelopes, hand address their envelopes in your own penmanship. Letters sent with mailing labels very seldom get read - or even opened.

Exercise 37

Go online and look for businesses who compliment yours. Email them and tell them that you believe an alliance between you would benefit both of you, or tell them that you believe they are really an expert in their area. Ask them appropriate questions and begin a relationship with them. List three of these businesses here.

If your business will really depend on internet advertising and your website, you must hit this hard and find people who you can connect with who have larger lists and who are not direct competitors. It is a good idea to have other things to sell on your website besides your own products. Decide to connect with a specific number of joint venture partners. In the beginning, you may want to find some products along the same market that you will be able to sell to your list as an affiliate. When doing this, it is really important to order the product first to be sure it is something you would be willing to put your name on. You can find these at http://www. commissionjunction.com . Otherwise, find some partners who you feel compliment your business and connect with them. List at least three of them here.

Think about a direct mail postcard that you could do promising a free report around something that your target market would be interested in learning about. It must be something really incredible that will make your market say "wow" at least five times. You may need to gather statistics to accomplish this. Write your 5 "wow"s here.

Indirect Contact

Advertising

This is the most expensive type of marketing you can do. This really needs to be done properly and the following needs to be well considered and executed:

- copy
- marketing
- design

My suggestion with advertising is to test carefully before you spend your family's future.

Advertising companies can be very good; however, they are also expensive. I believe that those companies that are willing to work for a percentage of the business generated are the only worthwhile companies. Don't deal with an advertising or marketing company who won't put their money where their mouth is.

I have a friend who was advertising his product during the 60s and 70s. He spent so much money on advertising that he opened his owner advertising agency. Obviously, you need to be huge to do something of this magnitude. It also saved him an enormous amount of money every year, since the advertising agency generally gets paid a percentage of the total advertising cost.

The list of advertising methods and all of the connotations that go along with them are endless. Advertising is only limited by the imaginations of business owners and advertising sales professionals who get their attention.

In my town one of the most used and efficient forms of advertising is done on the back and sides of buses used by the local Council on Aging. This has the unique advantage of also being partly tax deductible because it's considered a charitable contribution. If you can advertise and give to charity at the same time, you can enjoy the IRS benefits, although this is always subject to change.

There are a couple of issues around marketing by advertising, and although I know that it can sometimes be extremely profitable, it's only profitable if you get it right. There's a lot to get right.

First, we're assuming that you already know who your market is. Now you have to design copy that will appeal to those people. For that reason, advertising is only good if you have a product that will appeal to the masses. For instance, it's worth it for a tradesman to advertise because he can appeal to many different people because we all live somewhere and eventually that building will need something. However, if you're a personal trainer, you have a limited market and a limited amount of time. You can't spend a great deal of money so you must contain your advertising budget.

So it comes down to what you say when you advertise and where, when and how you advertise and to whom.

There are many different ways to advertise. One thing that I can tell you is that you will be approached by many companies and sales representatives all trying to sell you advertising. Ask them the following three questions:

What is your distribution?
Can you give me phone numbers for happy customers?
Who are your competitors and why are you better?

Print Advertising

This is an enormous category and includes display and classified ads in newspapers, newsletter, magazines, trade journals, fliers, menus, and event programs. You need to be extremely careful about placement of these ads. For example, the best place in a newspaper for an ad for a sports bar would be in the sports section of the newspaper. A good event program for this same sports bar might be at the dog track or in any sports program, depending on whether or not these venues had a bar of their own.

You also need to ask what the circulation of the publication will be, so that you can weigh the cost against the number of potential target clients. It's generally better to go into specialized publications where you will find your market. For example, the local children's dance studio would do well to advertise in the school publication. They can also sponsor a giveaway in the school for a specific event.

When you are doing print advertising, your headline should address the problem in just a few words. It should be powerful and grab the attention of your market. Your copy should explain that you have the answer.

Hire a good copywriter and graphic designer. They are worth their weight in gold for these projects. I've seen "do it yourself" ads that were obviously not professionally done and it's heartbreaking when the business owner realizes that he forgot some crucial information in the ad, like his phone number, or when he proofs it and doesn't realize that they transposed a couple of digits in the phone number or put the wrong date in the ad.

Internet Advertising

I am not talking about your website here. This is the advertising that you do on the web, which consists of web directories, pay per click ads, SEO work and banner ads.

Web directories are similar to the yellow pages except they are accessed on the Internet, and you don't need a phone number. Instead you need an email address or website. These days it is more effective than the local phone book since more and more people go to the Internet to find providers.

Pay per Click ads are the ones that you find on Google and the other search engines. When you do a search for a specific item, using a keyword, and the results pop up, the pay ads are either listed on top or to the right of the other results. You purchase as many "hits" per day as you can budget for and when someone clicks through on your ad, you are charged whether or not they buy. The theory is that the people who click through are generally interested in buying.

For years Search Engine Optimization has been one of those elusive things. Everyone wants to be found on the web, and companies have always been around who would promise you that they can get you to the top of the Google page. They would never make any guarantees that they could actually get you there, however. That made pay-per-click more valuable because if you paid the highest dollar for pay-per-click, you would have first place. However, as people have used the internet, they have become aware that just because someone is paying to have first place, doesn't mean that they are the best. Now they go past the paid placements and go to the first "organic" or natural placement on the search page. There are some great companies who will guarantee your placement on Google. If they won't make the guarantee, don't give them your business. Keep searching until you find the right company to help you.

Banner ads are small one or two line ads that are placed on someone else's web site. These have lost popularity over the last few years, but are still available on some websites. If they are interested in your product or service they can click on the ad to get to your site for more information. These are not as popular as they used to be. With so much on the net these days, most people suffer from search overwhelm. Unless it's a site where they go regularly, when they are taking their time and they know most of the content on that site and are therefore open to additional information, you may not get great response.

Audio/Video Advertising

Audio and video ads can be used in many different places - radio, television, and recently, on the internet. This applies not just to using audio on your website, but also to posting videos on you tube and other video social sites. A really good video can get you great play and can actually build your business the same way a good TV commercial works. It doesn't need to be more than a minute or too long. It's actually a disadvantage if it is too long.

If you want to learn more about doing your own videos, or want to pay someone to do it for you, the best place to start is by doing some research on the web. It is not very difficult to do your own videos, depending on the level of professionalism that you desire

If you want to do telephone presentations, you'll need a telephone conferencing system. You can get one for free at http://freeconferencecall. com . This will allow you to tape your teleclasses or presentations and reuse them. If you want better capabilities, and you want to have breakout sessions so you can give your customers an assignment that they can work on with another customer, then listen to how each of them completes the exercise, one that I am familiar with is Maestro Conference. You may find some that are better than these, since technology changes on a daily basis and just keeps getting better.

Exercise 38

Spend time systematically looking at all forms of advertising that you might use in your business. List some here.

Save ads that you like and make notes about why you like them.

Purchase and read the book "Ads That Sell".

Consider all forms of advertising before you make any decisions. Talk to other businesses that have used the different forms of advertising and ask them questions around why they use this form, how they developed their ads, and what they would recommend you do. Listen to all of these opinions before you decide to proceed with any advertising. Make a list of possible advertising places here after you do your research.

Decide what you will do to try to increase the popularity and the placement of your website. What methods will you use?

Natural Web Optimization

We've talked about the importance of putting up a good basic website, and we have talked about optimizing your site to get good Google placement. There are some things that we can do to naturally help a site to get good placement. These things are subject to change at any moment, so if some of them change, don't be surprised.

There are some basic things you can do to make this process easier and they won't cost you anything.

- Be sure to have your most important keyword or words in your domain name. This is really important and not always easy because so many good names are already being used.
- Be sure to come up with a very complete list of keywords that describe your business. Use them in your page titles
- Use your keywords in your copy on the appropriate pages.
- Place articles that you write, or that are written for you, on your pages. They should be   keyword rich, but used appropriately.

In the event you really want to work on giving your site great placement, I suggest talking to several SEO companies to see what is important at the time that you are ready to launch or re-launch your site. Unfortunately, as I said before, all SEO companies are not created equal. Some of them are using outdated strategies, which is probably why they are not being successful. Do some research on the web, listen to any new podcasts that can give you direction. The bottom line is that you can only feel comfortable with one that stands behind their work with a guarantee.

Exercise 39

Spend some time at Google ad words studying keywords that would be appropriate for your business. List them here.

Narrow your keywords to your market as much as possible, and look at the individual keyword cost. List some definite keywords to use here.

Add your keywords to your copy, your titles, and all of your pages. Get listed in both Yahoo.com and DMOZ Directory.

Connect your online articles to your site.

Buy some keywords from Google to test the results. Do it for a very limited time to be sure you are converting the "hits" to customers. Track your results here over a seven day period.

If your online presence is critical to your success, hire a Search Engine Optimization company to help you. Make a list of possible SEO companies and their costs.

Publicity

Anything that you do that hypes your company is considered publicity. If you are recognized for doing good works, or are interviewed about something related to your industry, you are getting great publicity. This is wonderful for your company because it gives the public a chance to see your company the way other people see you.

Press Releases

When you open your business you will want to formulate a press release. This is a kind of birth announcement where you are planting the "use my company" seed. This can be used many times during your business's lifetime as a way to keep your name in front of the public. You can use it anytime the following happens in your company
New Employee
Employee Promotion
Employee Award
New Product or Service

I'm sure that you can find even more examples if you are diligent and aware of the opportunities. These press releases should be sent to your local newspapers and publications, and online through the various publications.

For the primary press release, to announce the commencement of business, you will want to include the following:

Press Release headline – (online version use your keywords or keyword phrases)
Sub-Headline or Summary - Summarizes what is about to be said in the body of your press release.
Your city, Your state
Month, Day, Year
Quote from Owner
    Start talking about problems your target market is facing.
    How your product or service will help your target market
    solve their problem above.
If you have a website, then talk about why it is unique and what it provides. Talk about the owner and what gives you credibility to back up your product or service.
How you came out with the idea ?
Why you created the product after that?
Details about your company.
Details on how to access the product or service, for internet use domain address)
Contact info for publication:

Your Full Name
Founder, YourDomain.com
Phone
Email

These will announcements are not always going to be published. They are printed as space allows, but if you have a good contact at the particular publication where you sent it, you have a better chance of having it appear.

Online Networking and Social Sites

This category can be considered either direct or indirect, depending on whether you are doing the work yourself or not. For these purposes, I am going to assume that you are subcontracting this work, because it can be very time-consuming.

Social media is the new form of advertising. If Google is the yellow pages of the internet, then LinkedIn must be a billboard. There are many experts who can teach you how to use social media really well. I will give you the basics here.

Although I have just suggested that you will probably want to subcontract this to a professional, you must know is that personalization is extremely important in this arena. I might suggest that in the beginning you do this yourself. As time goes on, you can hire people to do this for you. You want to set it up so that it shows your personality, so that people can decide to like you, know you and begin to trust you. When you are in an area where you can talk about your expertise, such as Linked In, they will begin to respect your abilities and expertise, and that will really skyrocket your business.

The second thing that you need to know is that you need to limit the amount of time that you spend here every day. It is easy to get onto the web and disappear there for most of the day, which, although it is fun, is really not productive.

Whether you are part of the global community or the local community, register with all of the social media sites.

Start with http://facebook.com . This is a great starting place and you first need to register in your name. Build your list of friends. Tell them what's going on in your life. Be sure to add people with who you really have common interests. Add pictures as you can. Don't add all of your pictures at once. Add them just one or two a day. Although this area is just your personal area, it is an appropriate place to build a presence.

You can also reach out to prominent business people to begin a connection with them. If you want to have a relationship with someone who is much more successful than you are, this is a great way to begin that relationship.

Then, add a Facebook fan page for your company. This is the area where you will really start to talk about your business and expertise. You can carefully choose which of your friends that you want to tell about your fan page. You will also be able to announce specials for your business, events, etc. You may want to consider running a Facebook add to build up your fan page.

Then add http://Linkedin.com On this site, you want to concentrate on your business. Join groups that are relevant to what you do. Start discussions, update your events, and generally let everyone understand what you do best.

Linkedin is an extremely valuable site for any business that sells to other businesses. It is a great place to introduce your business to them so that you can get the word out about your particular area of expertise. You cannot just connect with anyone. You will need to join groups to get to know new people. If there is someone specific that you want to get to know, you can go to their Linkin profile, see what groups they are members of and join one of their groups. Alternatively, if you know someone who knows them, you can ask for an introduction.

Of course, you can add http://twitter.com . Twitter is a great place where you periodically update everyone who follows you about what you are doing. It needs to be less than 148 characters – about a sentence. There are so many things that you can do on twitter! The first is that you need to know that you don't have to sit at your computer all day and send Tweets. You can actually use a website called http://tweetlater.com and schedule your tweets ahead of time. At the time that I am writing this, the most effective times of day seem to be 9 AM, 1 PM, 6 PM and 10 PM EST. You also want to build your list of followers. Which you can do by going to http://twollo. com and choosing what your interests are. This site will automatically subscribe you to follow those people. Some of these people will follow you back. You can decide if you want to follow them or not. Although I don't recommend it, if you want to follow all of the people who follow you, you can go to http://dossy.org/twitter/karma and register there. Then you can pull up your entire list. You will have the option of separating these names into followers, following, or both. Choose following only, and check all at the bottom of the page. Then check bulk unsubscribe, and all of those who chose not to follow you will be deleted.

There is a caution here. If you build your list too quickly, without being sure that you have common interests, you will not have a good following, so you may want to forego the automation part of this. Personalization is the key to being successful in this arena.

Twitter is an important aspect of any type of marketing now. The local Chamber of Commerce members Twitter, as do many local business and employed people. It's great to announce successes and new products for your business – even specials that you're currently running. You just need to be careful to not spend your day there.

Ecademy.com is a great site. To really benefit from this one, you may want to upgrade from free to a paid membership. They have a really good active community.

Merchantcircle.com is a good site if you are looking for local business. This is a site where you'll find a lot of brick and mortar businesses as well as home based business people. It's great for building local connections.

Google plus is just coming online as I write this. It is predicted to eventually be bigger and better than Facebook. We'll keep an eye on how that progresses. It has some distinct advantages over Facebook, starting with the fact that you can put people in different circles, so you can separate out the people who see specific parts of what you write. That is head and shoulders above Facebook, and it will be interesting to see what other features they add as time goes on.

If you are strictly online, then you also need to go to both Google and Yahoo and find forums that pertain to your business. It's a great place to find people who are interested in what you have to say!

There are an unlimited number of online marketing masters who can help you with an online marketing campaign. This list grows on a daily basis. It was my intention to list some of them here, but there are so many, who have such specific areas of expertise that I decided to suggest that you Google online marketing help around whatever area you want help. Be careful! Some are great, some are scams. Find the ones who will give you a lot of really good free information before they ask for money. The only one that I really spend money with is Eben Pagan, who I've found to be extremely knowledgeable and very generous with his information.

Exercise 40

Sign up for all of your online social accounts, Facebook, Twitter, and LinkedIn, filling out your profile information thoroughly.

Get involved in the online communities to find your fit. Decide which your favorite is and list it here.

Invite friends to connect with you. List at least 15 here.

Keeping In Touch

Warning: Losing just one contact might cost you thousands of dollars in business.

Suppose this one contact would have become a good customer and would have used your service regularly over the years, if you had just kept in touch with them. They would have called you every time they needed your primary service. How much would that have cost you? Suppose that you eventually offered other services which built on your first service, but they never got to find out about them because you didn't keep in touch with them. How much would that have meant for your business?

Suppose this one contact would have sent you just three referrals who would have used you forever? Suppose this one contact would have sent you three referrals per year for the life of your business. How much would that have meant for your business? Suppose those referrals which you never got had each referred you to just two others? How much money would that have meant for your business?

The sad part is that if you don't keep in touch, you will never know.

It becomes even more important as time goes on to be sure that you have a means of going back to people, and reconnecting with them so that you aren't forgotten. I can't tell you how many clients have tried to remember the name of a client that they liked who put money in their pocket, yet they couldn't remember their name, and couldn't find it anywhere in their files.

After you first meet someone, you will want to send them something to remind them of who you are. For some, as soon as they have finished talking to you they will forget you unless you can remind them that you exist. How many times have you met someone, then forgot about them? If you haven't gotten a business card, you have absolutely no way to know who they are or how to reach them. I've had this experience many times, and it is sad when I get home and realize that I could have used their product or service, or I knew someone else who really needed whatever they had to offer and now I have no way of getting in touch with them. Drat!

Sometimes, you will meet someone who promises to call you and get more information from you. You believe that they were really interested. They weren't just humoring you or pretending to be interested. Yet you never hear from them and you don't know why.

If you follow up with them, you can fix this.

No matter what other strategies you use, it is critical to be sure to find ways to keep in touch with everyone that you meet. This is a daunting task, if you don't handle it from the beginning, and it will take commitment and organization to accomplish this. If you have good contact management software, it should be a piece of cake.
There are several ways to follow up:

- Telephone
- Email
- U.S. Mail
- In Person Visit to Their Business

Telephone Call

If you've agreed to call them at a specific time, that's great! If you haven't, realize that there are some times to call that are better than others. If you are calling a business owner, it is best to not call them first thing in the morning. Realize that they have a routine that they follow, and they are probably dealing with company issues/emergencies for the first part of their day. Call later in the morning to try to reach them.

When you call, either they will answer, or you will get a secretarial type of person. If you get them on the phone, introduce yourself, remind them of where you met, then ask them if this is a good time to call. This is really important because you want all of their attention, and if they are distracted or busy with something else, you don't want to launch into whatever you want to say. Allow them the opportunity to reschedule or to consider whether this is a good time for them. If it is not, let them suggest another time that will work better for them. Don't suggest that they call you back, because then they will need to write down your contact information, and if they are normal, they will scribble it on a piece of paper that may get lost and you will never hear from them again. Tell them that you understand and will be happy to call them back at a better time.

If you get a secretary or office person, ask if they are available. The office person will either put you through or ask to take a message. Tell the office person who you are, and that you are following up on a conversation that you had with this person on whatever day it was that you met them. This assures that the office person will give your contact the message, and if the contact doesn't remember you, he may call you just in case he is overlooking something important.

You can also ask the office person what the best time is in general to reach the contact. They usually have a good feel for the boss's schedule, and don't want to have to take another message from you. Avoid sounding like a salesperson. Convey that you are a colleague.

A telephone call can be very effective provided that you can get to them on the telephone. If it is someone who is very busy, you may not have a great deal of success reaching them easily. It is important to not let it go by the wayside if you don't reach them the first time. If they don't take your call, don't be defensive and think that they don't want to talk to you. Chances are good that they prioritize their activities, and their schedules are very full. If calling them doesn't produce the results that you are hoping for, you will have to try something else.

Email

Email is an extremely easy tool to use and just about everyone checks their email at least one a day. Business people generally check it more often, making it a good way to communicate. If this is the first time that you are emailing them, use the subject kine to say something like "it was great to meet you", then remind them of who you are, where you met, and what you talked about. It should be very personalized. I get lots of emails from people that I met an event and it is obvious that they don't remember me or where we actually met, and unless I can put a face or memory to that person, I delete them and don't respond. It is really easy to offend people through email, because we all know that it doesn't cost anything to send email and there is no real commitment involved in sending an email.

For this reason, it is not my favorite way to follow up with a new contact.

U.S. Mail

This is actually a great way to follow up, because it is rare that anyone actually sends anything by mail anymore. It will cost you the price of postage, but it will be well worth it. You can use standard cards, personalized blank cards, or anything else that you feel is appropriate. If you are really romancing someone specific, you may want to send them an article that you found that you thought they would appreciate. If you saw an article in the paper about them or their company, or their picture in an offline newspaper, send them the copy with your congratulations or whatever might be correct. They will appreciate the recognition.

Personal Visit

This is something that can be done if they have a bricks and mortar location, particularly if they are onsite specifically to meet and greet clients. Although you and I know that is not a great use of their time, many business owners don't realize this, and use their time to hang around their business. If this is the case with someone that you want to cement your relationship with, and they have the capability of being a high dollar client, then is worth your time to visit with them in person. It doesn't need to be a long visit. Just a quick hello on your way to somewhere else. Don't make it a project. It won't be the highest and best use of your time.

Let's look at all of the times you need to keep in touch and the possible methods to do that.

Initial introduction
  Thirty days later
    Every three months
Subscribe to your list
  Once or twice a month
Become a client
  After service is completed
    Every three months
When they send you a referral
Birthdays, anniversaries, etc.

Sound overwhelming? Relax. It can be very easy to do this.

There are a limited number of ways that you will keep in touch with them. It's just a matter of sorting them to know which is best for each one. After you sort them several times, it becomes almost an unconscious task, because there are only a certain number of possibilities. You will keep in touch either by mail, email, telephone or in person.

If you keep in touch by email, there is nothing to really think of. You send it and it is done. You can also get some online cards through American Greetings, but they tend to not be very business like and may not work well.

If you keep in touch by telephone, I would not suggest that you do this for an initial introduction, because you may spend a lot of time chasing them to get them on the phone. This works great once they either become a client or give you a referral.

If you keep in touch by mail, you need to remember to keep stamps and cards in stock so that you don't need to make a special trip for these items every time that you need it. If you run out of either, by the time you get around to restocking, you may forget someone. If you want to keep in touch by mail, I would suggest that you use a service called Send Out Cards. This is a great service where you can go online, choose your card out of a catalogue of about 100,000 cards. They will send your card for you through the United States mail and it is much less expensive than buying a card and mailing it yourself.

If you decide to keep in touch with them in person, it may be a special meeting or it might be in another group setting. This will be determined by the importance of the contact, and how you met them.

However you decide to communicate with them, you just need to determine whether they will either be future clients, current clients, past clients, referral sources, or tire kickers (the ones who never buy anything but read whatever information you give them that is free). There is nothing wrong with tire kickers, by the way, because they sometimes become referral sources, although you may never even know about that.

Back to the times you will communicate with them.

Initial introduction – When you first meet them, this will be the most time consuming of all of your communication. It means that you have to enter all of their information into your contact management software so you can keep track of them. You will want to decide what group to put them into, and you want to make as many notes about them as you can. In addition, you will want to send them something that is very personalized to remind them of who you are. You can either send them an email, which is quick, easy, and free, or you can send them a standard card or you can send a send out card.

Thirty days later, you will want to touch them again in some manner, just to reinforce your beginning relationship. If you are going to another event where you will see the same person, that's great. Problem solved and done. Three months later, and every quarter thereafter, you want to be sure to reach out to this person again. Out of sight, out of mind is extremely true in this case. They haven't formed any sort of affection or respect for you, so you need to keep your name in front of them. Just as you need to fertilize a plant, you need to cultivate your relationships.

New List Subscription – This is an easy one. When someone subscribes to your list, they will generally do so as the result of some sort of free report that you can offer them. You can make this offer on your website or through any type of advertising. As soon as they subscribe, you will send them a report that will be so packed with information that you will knock their socks off!

Then, on a bi-monthly or monthly basis, you should follow up with your Ezine, also known as a newsletter. We've already discussed the content for your Ezine, and it is a great way to keep up with all of your contacts. You can use a service like Aweber, which will allow you to have a series of Ezines preloaded, and they are sent out automatically from Ezine 1 to Ezine 100, and everyone gets each of these no matter when they subscribed. You can also just send the most recent one to everyone, or you can send one from the series and one recent one every month. That way you are sending two per month which is still not overwhelming. Do not send to your list daily! You will cause them to unsubscribe.

Become a Client – This should be a personalized email, phone call or mail piece, thanking them for becoming a client, and reinforcing the scope of the work that you will perform for them. This is an exciting time for you and a slightly scary time for the client. Although they trust you somewhat, they know that there is always a chance, even though it may be slight, that you won't perform as promised, so a little encouragement from you at this time is a good business practice.

When the work is completed, you should contact them again. At this time, I feel that a phone call is best, to be sure that they were satisfied with the service that they received. It is a great time for you to take your bow, if everything was done as excellently as it should be done. In the event that there was something amiss, this will give you the opportunity to fix it.

After the work has been done, you can do one of two things. You can either make them subscribers or you can email or mail to them every three months with special deals or events or whatever you are offering at that time.

Sending You a Referral – If someone sends you a referral, it is important to be effusive when it comes to thanking them. If you offer a spiff for giving you a referral, send it to them quickly. Don't drag your feet. If you haven't promised them anything, you still need to send them something, depending on the dollar value of the referral. Send Out Cards has small gifts that you can send. Many online companies have gifts that they will send for you. You should cater to the referral partner's likes and dislikes. Clearly you won't send chocolate to someone who hates candy, or a book to someone who sells books. At the very least, if it is a small dollar referral, you should send them a personalized card or call them.

Birthdays, anniversaries, etc. – It can be really cumbersome to send cards to everyone in your universe, unless you have clerical help to do this for you. If that's the case, let this person keep track of these special occasions. For non-clients, they can send them an email to say "Happy Whatever". If they are a client, you should send them a card through the mail, using Send out Cards. If they are referral partners who take good care of you, it is important to send them something to say thank you. Some businesses will buy promotional items that are specific to their company. They will give these out to clients, referral partners, and anyone else that they find deserving.

Exercise 41

What will be your primary form of keeping in touch with your clients?

If you have not been regularly keeping in touch, I would recommend that you start with your contacts from the last two weeks, as well as your clients and former clients. Touch them today in one using one of the four methods. List these clients here so that you will have a record of your starting point.

Chapter 8

Conclusion

Unlimited Possibilities Exist
Outside the Box

Imagination will get you everywhere. The things we've talked about here are just the tip of the iceberg. Spend some time thinking about what you can do to demonstrate your unique offering. Think as far outside the box as you can.

I have a marketing background, and I love imaginative marketing. Nothing makes me happier than seeing something really different being done – as long as it's well done and effective. In many cases, I'll get to know the professional who is being innovative just because I like to be around imaginative people.

Think about what you can do for your business. Here are some of the things that I find memorable enough to merit mention here.

I've seen a gourmet chef who owned a catering company had a man dressed like royalty carried in parade form on a reproduction of a Roman dais. He was placed somewhat ceremoniously near her show display and she and her counterpart fed him delicacies. The sign on the back of the man trailing the end of the parade said: "Follow me to see what we will do for you!" It brought the crowd and a lot of smiles.

A local orthodontist here in town sponsors the annual Halloween party for all the kids. Since that's a big candy holiday, he gives out plenty of candy and new toothbrushes.

If you are a business coach, you can dress as a referee with a whistle to attend an event. Use the whistle liberally. The attendees will never forget that you are a coach.

If you're a landscaper, send a potted rose plant to someone who allowed you to bid their job with a note that reads: "Hope you feel that we rose to the occasion. Thanks for the opportunity to meet with you."

A dog groomer could provide you with a professional picture of your dog right after he's groomed. This would be a joint venture between the groomer and the photographer and would benefit both, particularly if the photographer let the owner know that there are other photos of their pet available at a discounted price.

Accountants have given out notepads that look like dollars on one side except with a picture of them instead of George Washington and in the area where the In God We Trust is, they have their name and phone number.

The caveat here, of course is that although all of these things can make you initially memorable, this is not the answer to getting long term clients. This is just a way to get your foot in the door. It is only the beginning.

Now you have to show 'em what you got! What will really get you clients for life is a great service that is unique and provides great value, combined with some enthusiastic marketing to make sure that everyone knows what you have to offer.

It's so important to be just as imaginative about the Bullseye Market that you choose as you are about the rest of your marketing!

Wrapping It Up With a Big Red Bow

By now, if you've done the exercises along the way, you should have a great business and marketing plan, and a great service business that is unique in its approach and provides great value – value that your customer knows he can only get from you. These are the companies that everyone wants. It's the reason that everyone likes rock stars who write their own songs, and companies like Google and Twitter, who are one of a kind.

It's my hope that if you take away nothing else from this book, you take away the element of **unique proposition**. That is, if you can offer your market something that no one else can or has, even if it is a small market, you will have all of their business. You can survive quite well on that small market because they will be willing to pay to have a service tailored to their specific need.

As I was writing this book, I went back to visit my hometown in Pennsylvania which is a very ethnic area. There are large populations of Irish, Italian, and Polish people. I went to a local church picnic. There were three food stands. One for hot dogs, hamburgers, etc. One for pizza, fries, and different types of sandwiches. The third one sold nothing but potato pancakes. Guess which one was busiest? If you said potato pancakes, you were correct. I waited in line for 45 minutes to get 3 greasy, wonderful potato pancakes, paying either a dollar a piece or 3 for $2.50. There were no lines at either of the other stands.

If you have the only game in town, even if your customer doesn't like your personality, if he knows you can solve his problem, he will be your best friend and pay you to give him information. Remember the days when you had to send mail through the post office? Everyone hated the post office, but you had no choice. If you wanted to send something, you had to use it.

In my town, rather than hiring more customer service people because they were so busy, my post office instituted a take a number system and put chairs in the lobby. That's the kind of arrogance that the only fish in the sea can have. They didn't need to worry about the quality of their service or whether you liked them. They could do whatever they wanted and we had to like it.

Joe Polish started his career in online marketing by teaching carpet cleaners how to market themselves. Carpet cleaners! He's now one of the most well-known and respected Internet marketers anywhere. He now appeals to all Internet marketers, which is a much larger market than carpet cleaners. He can do that because he built a successful reputation teaching what he knew.

What he taught us is my final gift to you. That is this:

Corner your Bullseye Market by concentrating on the one issue you can solve for them. When you've conquered that market and you are known as being the expert in that arena, then you can find another Bulls eye Market, maybe even more lucrative than the last. You'll have choices - you can keep doing that first thing, if you want to, OR you can sell it to someone who has basic skills but not the knowledge that you have. Someone who needs to buy something already set up and systematized. Someone who doesn't have the marketing skills that you have in your possession now that you've finished this book. I truly hope that I have given you the Miracle Grow that you need for your business, and moved you from Survival to Success, which is my personal goal for you.

In Your Service,

Luann Allen
http://www.successfanatic.com

Author's Late Addition

As I was about to publish this book, I had a meeting with a group of Service Business Owners who reminded me of a difficult situation for many of them.

It's such a common problem that is easily solved in my Fee, Fi(nances), Fo(r), Fum(bling) Professionals course that I didn't include it when writing this book.

The problem is how to get paid for your work after it has been completed. In this economy it is even more critical. Many times people will look for any sign that the service wasn't perfectly performed so they can either refuse to pay, or ask for a discount. If you are an extreme expert that they will need again, they will pay you, although they may delay payment just because their money is tight. If you are providing a service that they may not need again, you may wait for a long time to get paid, if you get paid at all.

There are a couple of ways to take care of this.

One, if you are a technical or mechanical service professional, like an electrician or plumber, you can require a credit card to guarantee payment BEFORE you even go on the service call. In some instances, if they are happy with your service, they may ask you to store their credit card information. DON'T DO THAT. Storing their information gives you liability if they suffer identity theft, and you don't want to be in that position.

When you take their credit card information, you can tell them that you will send them an invoice and charge their card when the service has been completed. If they don't want you to charge their card, they have the option of paying the service man when he is there.

Two, if you are an accountant, a coach, a consultant, or any of a number of other high end professionals, you can make sure that you take at least half of your fee before you begin, and require payments along the way. For a coach, it is easy to explain that payment is part of their commitment to you and they must be sure to pay you on time so you can pay your bills in a timely manner. If you are a coach and they are unwilling to commit to payment, they will also not commit to doing all of the work they need to do. This is one of many "tells" that you can use to understand their determination and character.

You can arrange a PayPal account or a credit card account to make it easy for them. There is no charge involved in setting up a PayPal account. You can also set up a merchant account either with your bank or online. Just shop for the lowest rates if you choose to go with a merchant account.

Never take a client without knowing how you will get paid. Your number one responsibility is to yourself and your family. I know that sounds harsh, but if you don't get paid, you won't be able to take care of ANY of your clients, and that isn't fair to your other clients.

This may sound harsh to many of you. It is not as harsh as turning over an account to a collection agency or having to tell your own creditors that you can't pay them. You must be proactive and handle this before it becomes an issue. To some extent, it is a way to train your clients. After the first time, they won't blink when you ask for prepayment because they will expect it and have their credit card in their hand when they call you. After all, they are most willing to pay when they need to solve the problem.

Following this system will keep you in the black.

If you want to take my Fee, Fi, Fo, Fum Financial Course, please contact me.

Luann